Published by the WHITE HOUSE HISTORICAL ASSOCIATION
With the cooperation of the NATIONAL GEOGRAPHIC SOCIETY, Washington, D. C.

The First Ladies

By Margaret Brown Klapthor

THE FIRST LADIES

By *Margaret Brown Klapthor*, Curator Emeritus, Division of Political History, National Museum of American History, Smithsonian Institution

PRODUCED BY THE NATIONAL GEOGRAPHIC SOCIETY AS A PUBLIC SERVICE
Gilbert M. Grosvenor, President and Chairman of the Board
Reg Murphy, Executive Vice President
Michela A. English, Senior Vice President
PREPARED BY THE BOOK DIVISION
William R. Gray, Vice President and Director
Charles Kogod, Assistant Director
STAFF FOR THE FIRST EDITION:
Mary Ann Harrell, Managing Editor
Susan C. Burns, Jennifer Urquhart, Researchers
Geraldine Linder, Picture Editor
Ursula Perrin Vosseler, Art Director
PHOTOGRAPHY: *Steve Adams, Joseph H. Bailey, Sean Baldwin, J. Bruce Baumann, Victor R. Boswell, Jr., David S. Boyer, Sisse Brimberg, Nelson H. Brown, Dan J. Dry, Thomas Hooper, Larry D. Kinney, Erik Kvalsvik, Bates Littlehales, George F. Mobley, Robert S. Oakes, Martin Rogers, James E. Russell, Joseph J. Scherschel, David Valdez, Volkmar Wentzel*
STAFF FOR THE EIGHTH EDITION: *Jane H. Buxton*, Managing Editor; *Richard M. Crum*, Text Editor; *Melanie Patt-Corner*, Researcher; *Elizabeth G. Jevons, Sandra F. Lotterman, Peggy J. Oxford*, Staff Assistants
MANUFACTURING AND QUALITY MANAGEMENT: *George V. White*, Director; *Robert W. Messer*, Manager; *Clifton M. Brown III*, Assistant Manager/Film Archivist

White House staff members who assisted in the preparation of this edition: *Rex Scouten*, Curator; *Betty Monkman*, Associate Curator; *William Allman*, Assistant Curator; *Lydia S. Tederick*, Curatorial Assistant

First Lady Caroline Harrison, who enjoyed painting for recreation, created watercolors such as Flowering Dogwood. *She also held china-painting classes at the White House.*

COVER: *Portrait of Martha Washington, painted by Eliphalet F. Andrews in 1878, hangs in the East Room of the White House as a companion piece for the Gilbert Stuart portrait of her husband.*
PAGE 1: *Hand-colored engraving* The President's House, Washington *gives an idyllic view of the White House during the Jacksonian age, around 1833.*
PAGES 2-3: *George and Martha Washington appear at right in an unknown artist's painting "Reception at Mount Vernon." Its style suggests a fictionalized illustration for a 19th-century popular magazine. Previously unpublished, the painting hangs in the headquarters of the National Society of the Daughters of the American Revolution, in Washington, D. C., on loan from the Rhode Island Society.*

Foreword

The American people have made the role of First Lady one of the most important jobs in the country. It happened because each First Lady from Martha Washington onward contributed to her husband's historical reputation. It is a tribute to American women that, coming from different social and economic backgrounds, from many different geographical regions, and with diverse educational preparation, each First Lady served our country so well. Each left her own mark, and each teaches us something special about our history.

The White House Historical Association has published *The First Ladies* to give us an opportunity to know these fascinating women better. The biographies were written by Margaret B. Klapthor, Curator Emeritus of the Smithsonian Institution. Mrs. Klapthor has spent 50 years studying our First Ladies, and her findings put each woman into perspective. She highlights their individual achievements as well as the qualities that make them similar. As we learn about them, we begin to see that these women usually reflect the time in which they lived, so much so that a look at their lives becomes a panorama of women's history in America. Managing the social life at the White House and the personal welfare of the President and their families, the First Ladies set a standard for the women of their day. In addition, they brought their own interests to the same wide audience.

From the relative obscurity of the earliest First Ladies, a few shine like stars. We see Abigail Adams passionate in her love for John Adams, in her patriotism, and in her political and social beliefs. Dolley Madison dazzles Washington with her social skills and also proves to be an especially astute politician who aids her husband's presidential activities. Sarah Polk also assists her husband's political career. Acting as the President's private secretary, she enjoys politics more than entertaining.

The period beginning with the Civil War brought First Ladies who saw in their role an opportunity for service to the less fortunate. Mary Todd Lincoln spent hours visiting with wounded Civil War soldiers. Lucy Webb Hayes deeply touched the nation with her compassion for the poor and less privileged. Edith Roosevelt sewed for the needy.

With the 20th century, the role of First Lady included women with professional careers. Ellen Wilson was an accomplished artist; Grace Goodhue Coolidge taught the deaf; and Lou Henry Hoover was a geologist. Others, such as Eleanor Roosevelt, used their positions to speak out for peace, justice, equality for women, and "the needs of the common people."

I take courage from reading *The First Ladies*, and I hope that, like me, all of you who read these brief profiles will be motivated to learn more about this interesting group of Americans.

Hillary Rodham Clinton

In the East Room of the White House, President Abraham Lincoln greets Gen. Ulysses S. Grant, who presents his wife. To the President's left, Mary Todd Lincoln turns toward Gen. Winfield Scott, a military hero since the War of 1812. This detail from an oil painting of around 1867 draws on the actual chamber to portray an imaginary reception and famous persons of the times.

Contents

Martha Dandridge Custis Washington
1731-1802

"I think I am more like a state prisoner than anything else, there is certain bounds set for me which I must not depart from. . . ." So in one of her few surviving letters, Martha Washington confided to a niece that she did not entirely enjoy her role as first of First Ladies. She once conceded that "many younger and gayer women would be extremely pleased" in her place; she would "much rather be at home."

But when George Washington took his oath of office in New York City on April 30, 1789, and assumed the new duties of President of the United States, his wife brought to their position a tact and discretion developed over 58 years of life in Tidewater Virginia society.

Oldest daughter of John and Frances Dandridge, she was born June 2, 1731, on a plantation near Williamsburg. Typical for a girl in an 18th-century family, her education was almost negligible except in domestic and social skills, but she learned all the arts of a well-ordered household and how to keep a family contented.

As a girl of 18—about five feet tall, dark-haired, gentle of manner—she married the wealthy Daniel Parke Custis. Two babies died; two were hardly past infancy when her husband died in 1757.

From the day Martha married George Washington in 1759, her great concern was the comfort and happiness of her husband and her children. When his career led him to the battlegrounds of the Revolutionary War and finally to the Presidency, she followed him bravely. Her love of private life equaled her husband's; but, as she wrote to her friend Mercy Otis Warren, "I cannot blame him for having acted according to his ideas of duty in obeying the voice of his country." As for herself, "I am still determined to be cheerful and to be happy, in whatever situation I may be; for I have also learned from experience that the greater part of our happiness or misery depends upon our dispositions, and not upon our circumstances."

At the President's House in temporary capitals, New York and Philadelphia, the Washingtons chose to entertain in formal style, deliberately emphasizing the new republic's wish to be accepted as the equal of the established governments of Europe. Still, Martha's warm hospitality made her guests feel welcome and put strangers at ease. She took little satisfaction in "formal compliments and empty ceremonies," and declared that "I am fond only of what comes from the heart." Abigail Adams, who sat at her right during parties and receptions, praised her as "one of those unassuming characters which create Love & Esteem."

In 1797 the Washingtons said farewell to public life and returned to their beloved Mount Vernon, to live surrounded by kinfolk, friends, and a constant stream of guests eager to pay their respects to the celebrated couple. Martha's daughter Patsy had died at 17, her son Jack at 26, but Jack's children figured in the household. After George Washington died in 1799, Martha assured a final privacy by burning their letters; she died of a "severe fever" on May 22, 1802. Both lie buried at Mount Vernon, where Washington himself had planned an unpretentious tomb for them.

"Dear Patsy" to her husband, Martha Washington had this miniature painted by Charles Willson Peale about 1776; through the rest of the Revolutionary War, the general wore it in a gold locket. "Lady Washington," some admiring Americans called her; in a modest reference to her domestic skill, she described herself as an "old-fashioned Virginia house-keeper." "A most becoming pleasentness sits upon her countanance...," wrote Abigail Adams in 1789.

Abigail Adams considered it beneath her dignity to be painted bareheaded, so she chose a demure cap when she sat for this likeness, rendered by Gilbert Stuart— one of the young Republic's finest portraitists. The canvas depicts Mrs. Adams in 1800 at age 56. A few days after Stuart sketched her, she received the following written comments from a friend: "Your likeness has attracted . . . as many admirers as spectators. Stewart [sic] says, he wishes to god, he could have taken Mrs. Adams when she was young, he believes he should have a perfect Venus." When President Adams learned of this remark, he wholeheartedly agreed.

Abigail Smith Adams
1744-1818

Inheriting New England's strongest traditions, Abigail Smith was born in 1744 at Weymouth, Massachusetts. On her mother's side she was descended from the Quincys, a family of great prestige in the colony; her father and other forebears were Congregational ministers, leaders in a society that held its clergy in high esteem.

Like other women of the time, Abigail lacked formal education; but her curiosity spurred her keen intelligence, and she read avidly the books at hand. Reading created a bond between her and young John Adams, Harvard graduate launched on a career in law, and they were married in 1764. It was a marriage of the mind and of the heart, enduring for more than half a century, enriched by time.

The young couple lived on John's small farm at Braintree or in Boston as his practice expanded. In ten years she bore three sons and two daughters; she looked after family and home when he went traveling as circuit judge. "Alass!" she wrote in December 1773, "How many snow banks devide thee and me. . . ."

Long separations kept Abigail from her husband while he served the country they loved, as delegate to the Continental Congress, envoy abroad, elected officer under the Constitution. Her letters—pungent, witty, and vivid, spelled just as she spoke— detail her life in times of revolution. They tell the story of the woman who stayed at home to struggle with wartime shortages and inflation; to run the farm with a minimum of help; to teach four children when formal education was interrupted. Most of all, they tell of her loneliness without her "dearest Friend." That "one single expression," she said, "dwelt upon my mind and playd about my Heart. . . ."

In 1784, she joined him at his diplomatic post in Paris, and observed with interest the manners of the French. After 1785, she filled the difficult role of wife of the first United States Minister to Great Britain, and did so with dignity and tact. They returned happily in 1788 to Massachusetts and the handsome house they had just acquired in Braintree, later called Quincy, home for the rest of their lives.

As wife of the first Vice President, Abigail became a good friend to Mrs. Washington and a valued help in official entertaining, drawing on her experience of courts and society abroad. After 1791, however, poor health forced her to spend as much time as possible in Quincy. Illness or trouble found her resolute; as she once declared, she would "not forget the blessings which sweeten life."

When John Adams was elected President, she continued a formal pattern of entertaining—even in the primitive conditions she found at the new capital in November 1800. The city was wilderness, the President's House far from completion. Her private complaints to her family provide blunt accounts of both, but for her three months in Washington she duly held her dinners and receptions.

The Adamses retired to Quincy in 1801, and for 17 years enjoyed the companionship that public life had long denied them. Abigail died in 1818, and is buried beside her husband in United First Parish Church. She leaves her country a most remarkable record as patriot and First Lady, wife of one President and mother of another.

Jefferson's daughter Martha ("Patsy") posed for this oil-on-ivory miniature in 1789, at age 17; "a delicate likeness of her father," a friend called her during the White House years when she sometimes served as his hostess. Of her mother, whose name she bore, no portrait of any kind has survived.

Martha Wayles Skelton Jefferson
1748-1782

When Thomas Jefferson came courting, Martha Wayles Skelton at 22 was already a widow, an heiress, and a mother whose firstborn son would die in early childhood. Family tradition says that she was accomplished and beautiful—with slender figure, hazel eyes, and auburn hair—and wooed by many. Perhaps a mutual love of music cemented the romance; Jefferson played the violin, and one of the furnishings he ordered for the home he was building at Monticello was a "forte-piano" for his bride.

They were married on New Year's Day, 1772, at the bride's plantation home "The Forest," near Williamsburg. When they finally reached Monticello in a late January snowstorm to find no fire, no food, and the servants asleep, they toasted their new home with a leftover half-bottle of wine and "song and merriment and laughter." That night, on their own mountaintop, the love of Thomas Jefferson and his bride seemed strong enough to endure any adversity.

The birth of their daughter Martha in September increased their happiness. Within ten years the family gained five more children. Of them all, only two lived to grow up: Martha, called Patsy, and Mary, called Maria or Polly.

The physical strain of frequent pregnancies weakened Martha Jefferson so gravely that her husband curtailed his political activities to stay near her. He served in Virginia's House of Delegates and as governor, but he refused an appointment by the Continental Congress as a commissioner to France. Just after New Year's Day, 1781, a British invasion forced Martha to flee the capital in Richmond with a baby girl a few weeks old—who died in April. In June the family barely escaped an enemy raid on Monticello. She bore another daughter the following May, and never regained a fair measure of strength. Jefferson wrote on May 20 that her condition was dangerous. After months of tending her devotedly, he noted in his account book for September 6, "My dear wife died this day at 11-45 A.M."

Apparently he never brought himself to record their life together; in a memoir he referred to ten years "in unchequered happiness." Half a century later his daughter Martha remembered his sorrow: "the violence of his emotion... to this day I dare not describe to myself." For three weeks he had shut himself in his room, pacing back and forth until exhausted. Slowly that first anguish spent itself. In November he agreed to serve as commissioner to France, eventually taking "Patsy" with him in 1784 and sending for "Polly" later.

When Jefferson became President in 1801, he had been a widower for 19 years. He had become as capable of handling social affairs as political matters. Occasionally he called on Dolley Madison for assistance. And it was Patsy—now Mrs. Thomas Mann Randolph, Jr.—who appeared as the lady of the President's House in the winter of 1802-1803, when she spent seven weeks there. She was there again in 1805-1806, and gave birth to a son named for James Madison, the first child born in the White House. It was Martha Randolph with her family who shared Jefferson's retirement at Monticello until he died there in 1826.

Dolley Payne Todd Madison
1768-1849

For half a century she was the most important woman in the social circles of America. To this day she remains one of the best known and best loved ladies of the White House—though often referred to, mistakenly, as Dorothy or Dorothea.

She always called herself Dolley; and by that name the New Garden Monthly Meeting of the Society of Friends, in piedmont North Carolina, recorded her birth to John and Mary Coles Payne, settlers from Virginia. In 1769 John Payne took his family back to his home colony, and in 1783 he moved them to Philadelphia, city of the Quakers. Dolley grew up in the strict discipline of the Society, but nothing muted her happy personality and her warm heart.

John Todd, Jr., a lawyer, exchanged marriage vows with Dolley in 1790. Just three years later he died in a yellow-fever epidemic, leaving his wife with a small son.

By this time Philadelphia had become the capital city. With her charm and her laughing blue eyes, fair skin, and black curls, the young widow attracted distinguished attention. Before long Dolley was reporting to her best friend that "the great little Madison has asked. . . . to see me this evening."

Although Representative James Madison of Virginia was 17 years her senior, and Episcopalian in background, they were married in September 1794. The marriage, though childless, was notably happy; "our hearts understand each other," she assured him. He could even be patient with Dolley's son, Payne, who mishandled his own affairs—and, eventually, mismanaged Madison's estate.

Discarding the somber Quaker dress after her second marriage, Dolley chose the finest of fashions. Margaret Bayard Smith, chronicler of early Washington social life, wrote: "She looked a Queen. . . . It would be *absolutely impossible* for any one to behave with more perfect propriety than she did."

Blessed with a desire to please and a willingness to be pleased, Dolley made her home the center of society when Madison began, in 1801, his eight years as Jefferson's Secretary of State. She assisted at the White House when the President asked her help in receiving ladies, and presided at the first inaugural ball in Washington when her husband became Chief Executive in 1809.

Dolley's social graces made her famous. Her political acumen, prized by her husband, is less renowned, though her gracious tact smoothed many a quarrel. Hostile statesmen, difficult envoys from Spain or Tunisia, warrior chiefs from the west, flustered youngsters—she always welcomed everyone. Forced to flee from the White House by a British army during the War of 1812, she returned to find the mansion in ruins. Undaunted by temporary quarters, she entertained as skillfully as ever.

At their plantation Montpelier in Virginia, the Madisons lived in pleasant retirement until he died in 1836. She returned to the capital in the autumn of 1837, and friends found tactful ways to supplement her diminished income. She remained in Washington until her death in 1849, honored and loved by all. The delightful personality of this unusual woman is a cherished part of her country's history.

Already a hostess of outstanding success, Dolley Madison sat for this portrait by Gilbert Stuart in 1804. As wife of the Secretary of State, she began her long career of official hospitality; she sustained it for eight years as First Lady. Her manners, said a contemporary, "would disarm envy itself." Widowed, impoverished, and old, she never lost her charm or dignity; she enjoyed the deepening respect of her friends and country to the last.

Invariably elegant, Elizabeth Monroe chose an ermine scarf to complement her black velvet Empire-style gown for this portrait attributed to John Vanderlyn. Although she had traveled with her husband on diplomatic missions, delicate health limited her activities – and enjoyment – in her eight years as First Lady.

Elizabeth Kortright Monroe
1768-1830

Romance glints from the little that is known of Elizabeth Kortright's early life. She was born in New York City in 1768, daughter of an old New York family. Her father, Lawrence, had served the Crown by privateering during the French and Indian War and made a fortune. He took no active part in the War of Independence; and James Monroe wrote to his friend Thomas Jefferson in Paris in 1786 that he had married the daughter of a gentleman "injured in his fortunes" by the Revolution.

Strange choice, perhaps, for a patriot veteran with political ambitions and little money of his own; but Elizabeth was beautiful, and love was decisive. They were married in February 1786, when the bride was not yet 18.

The young couple planned to live in Fredericksburg, Virginia, where Monroe began his practice of law. His political career, however, kept them on the move as the family increased by two daughters and a son who died in infancy.

In 1794, Elizabeth Monroe accompanied her husband to France when President Washington appointed him United States Minister. Arriving in Paris in the midst of the French Revolution, she took a dramatic part in saving Lafayette's wife, imprisoned and expecting death on the guillotine. With only her servants in her carriage, the American Minister's wife went to the prison and asked to see Madame Lafayette. Soon after this hint of American interest, the prisoner was set free. The Monroes became very popular in France, where the diplomat's lady received the affectionate name of *la belle Américaine*.

For 17 years Monroe, his wife at his side, alternated between foreign missions and service as governor or legislator of Virginia. They made the plantation of Oak Hill their home after he inherited it from an uncle, and appeared on the Washington scene in 1811 when he became Madison's Secretary of State.

Elizabeth Monroe was an accomplished hostess when her husband took the Presidential oath in 1817. Through much of the administration, however, she was in poor health and curtailed her activities. Wives of the diplomatic corps and other dignitaries took it amiss when she decided to pay no calls — an arduous social duty in a city of widely scattered dwellings and unpaved streets.

Moreover, she and her daughter Eliza changed White House customs to create the formal atmosphere of European courts. Even the White House wedding of her daughter Maria was private, in "the New York style" rather than the expansive Virginia social style made popular by Dolley Madison. A guest at the Monroes' last levee, on New Year's Day in 1825, described the First Lady as "regal-looking" and noted details of interest: "Her dress was superb black velvet; neck and arms bare and beautifully formed; her hair in puffs and dressed high on the head and ornamented with white ostrich plumes; around her neck an elegant pearl necklace. Though no longer young, she is still a very handsome woman."

In retirement at Oak Hill, Elizabeth Monroe died on September 23, 1830; and family tradition says that her husband burned the letters of their life together.

Louisa Catherine Johnson Adams
1775-1852

Only First Lady born outside the United States, Louisa Catherine Adams did not come to this country until four years after she had married John Quincy Adams. Political enemies sometimes called her English. She was born in London to an English mother, Catherine Nuth Johnson, but her father was American—Joshua Johnson, of Maryland—and he served as United States consul after 1790.

A career diplomat at 27, accredited to the Netherlands, John Quincy developed his interest in charming 19-year-old Louisa when they met in London in 1794. Three years later they were married, and went to Berlin in course of duty. At the Prussian court she displayed the style and grace of a diplomat's lady; the ways of a Yankee farm community seemed strange indeed in 1801 when she first reached the country of which she was a citizen. Then began years divided among the family home in Quincy, Massachusetts, their house in Boston, and a political home in Washington, D. C. When the Johnsons had settled in the capital, Louisa felt more at home there than she ever did in New England.

She left her two older sons in Massachusetts for education in 1809 when she took two-year-old Charles Francis to Russia, where Adams served as Minister. Despite the glamour of the tsar's court, she had to struggle with cold winters, strange customs, limited funds, and poor health; an infant daughter born in 1811 died the next year. Peace negotiations called Adams to Ghent in 1814 and then to London. To join him, Louisa had to make a forty-day journey across war-ravaged Europe by coach in winter; roving bands of stragglers and highwaymen filled her with "unspeakable terrors" for her son. Happily, the next two years gave her an interlude of family life in the country of her birth.

Appointment of John Quincy as Monroe's Secretary of State brought the Adamses to Washington in 1817, and Louisa's drawing room became a center for the diplomatic corps and other notables. Good music enhanced her Tuesday evenings at home, and theater parties contributed to her reputation as an outstanding hostess.

But the pleasure of moving to the White House in 1825 was dimmed by the bitter politics of the election and by her own poor health. She suffered from deep depression. Though she continued her weekly "drawing rooms," she preferred quiet evenings—reading, composing music and verse, playing her harp. The necessary entertainments were always elegant, however; and her cordial hospitality made the last official reception a gracious occasion although her husband had lost his bid for re-election and partisan feeling still ran high.

Louisa thought she was retiring to Massachusetts permanently, but in 1831 her husband began 17 years of notable service in the House of Representatives. The Adamses could look back on a secure happiness as well as many trials when they celebrated their fiftieth wedding anniversary at Quincy in 1847. He was fatally stricken at the Capitol the following year; she died in Washington in 1852, and today lies buried at his side in the family church at Quincy.

"Try as she might, the Madam could never be Bostonian, and it was her cross in life," wrote Henry Adams of his London-born grandmother. Nor did Louisa Johnson Adams feel at ease in what she called the "Bull Bait" of Washington's political life. Gilbert Stuart painted her portrait in 1821.

With the devotion that always marked their marriage, Andrew Jackson once assured Rachel: "recollection never fails me of your likeness." Nearly heartbroken by her death, he wore a miniature of her daily and kept it on his bedside table every night. Family tradition held that the portrait above was the very memento he carried, and attributed it to Anna C. Peale. Current scholarship identifies it as the work of Louisa Catherine Strobel, who was in France from 1815 to 1830; she probably copied a study from life, for one of "Aunt Rachel's" relatives.

Rachel Donelson Jackson
1767-1828

·

Wearing the white dress she had purchased for her husband's inaugural ceremonies in March 1829, Rachel Donelson Jackson was buried in the garden at The Hermitage, her home near Nashville, Tennessee, on Christmas Eve in 1828. Lines from her epitaph —"A being so gentle and so virtuous slander might wound, but could not dishonor" —reflected his bitterness at campaign slurs that seemed to precipitate her death.

Rachel Donelson was a child of the frontier. Born in Virginia, she journeyed to the Tennessee wilderness with her parents when only 12. At 17, while living in Kentucky, she married Lewis Robards, of a prominent Mercer County family. His unreasoning jealousy made it impossible for her to live with him; in 1790 they separated, and she heard that he was filing a petition for divorce.

Andrew Jackson married her in 1791; and after two happy years they learned to their dismay that Robards had not obtained a divorce, only permission to file for one. Now he brought suit on grounds of adultery. After the divorce was granted, the Jacksons quietly remarried in 1794. They had made an honest mistake, as friends well understood, but whispers of adultery and bigamy followed Rachel as Jackson's career advanced in both politics and war. He was quick to take offense at, and ready to avenge, any slight to her.

Scandal aside, Rachel's unpretentious kindness won the respect of all who knew her—including innumerable visitors who found a comfortable welcome at The Hermitage. Although the Jacksons never had children of their own, they gladly opened their home to the children of Rachel's many relatives. In 1809 they adopted a nephew and named him Andrew Jackson, Jr. They also reared other nephews; one, Andrew Jackson Donelson, eventually married his cousin Emily, one of Rachel's favorite nieces.

Jackson's hostess Emily Donelson: by his friend and portraitist Ralph E. W. Earl.

When Jackson was elected President, he planned to have young Donelson for private secretary, with Emily as company for Rachel. After losing his beloved wife he asked Emily to serve as his hostess.

Though only 21 when she entered the White House, she skillfully cared for her uncle, her husband, four children (three born at the mansion), many visiting relatives, and official guests. Praised by contemporaries for her wonderful tact, she had the courage to differ with the President on issues of principle. Frail throughout her lifetime, Emily died of tuberculosis in 1836.

During the last months of the administration, Sarah Yorke Jackson, wife of Andrew Jackson, Jr., presided at the mansion in her stead.

Hannah Hoes Van Buren
1783-1819

Cousins in a close-knit Dutch community, Hannah Hoes and Martin Van Buren grew up together in Kinderhook, New York. Evidently he wanted to establish his law practice before marrying his sweetheart—they were not wed until 1807, when he was 24 and his bride just three months younger. Apparently their marriage was a happy one, though little is known of Hannah as a person.

Van Buren omitted even her name from his autobiography; a gentleman of that day would not shame a lady by public references. A niece who remembered "her loving, gentle disposition" emphasized "her modest, even timid manner." Church records preserve some details of her life; she seems to have considered formal church affiliation a matter of importance.

Angelica Singleton Van Buren: daughter-in-law and hostess of the widower President.

She bore a son in Kinderhook, three others in Hudson, where Martin served as county surrogate; but the fourth son died in infancy. In 1816 the family moved to the state capital in Albany. Soon the household included Martin's law partner and three apprentices; relatives came and went constantly, and Hannah could return their visits. Contemporary letters indicate that she was busy, sociable, and happy. She gave birth to a fifth boy in January 1817.

But by the following winter her health was obviously failing, apparently from tuberculosis. Not yet 36, she died on February 5, 1819. The Albany *Argus* called her "an ornament of the Christian faith."

Her husband never remarried; he moved into the White House in 1837 as a widower with four bachelor sons. Now accustomed to living in elegant style, he immediately began to refurbish a mansion shabby from public use under Jackson. Across Lafayette Square, Dolley Madison reigned as matriarch of Washington society; when her young relative-by-marriage Angelica Singleton came up from South Carolina for a visit, Dolley took her to the White House to pay a call.

Angelica's aristocratic manners, excellent education, and handsome face won the heart of the President's eldest son, Abraham. They were married in November 1838; next spring a honeymoon abroad polished her social experience. Thereafter, while Abraham served as the President's private secretary, Angelica presided as lady of the house. The only flaw in her pleasure in this role was the loss of a baby girl. Born at the White House, she lived only a few hours. In later years, though spending much time in South Carolina and in Europe, Angelica and her husband made their home in New York City; she died there in 1878.

"Jannetje," Martin Van Buren called his wife, in the Dutch language of their ancestors. An unknown artist painted two portraits of her: one for her husband, one for her niece Maria Hoes Cantine. Initials on the back of the gold brooch indicate that this belonged to the niece; an inset holds a plaited lock of reddish-brown hair, probably a memento of "Aunt Hannah." Prolonged illness, almost certainly tuberculosis, claimed Hannah Van Buren at age 35: years later, Maria remembered "the perfect composure" of her deathbed farewell to her children, and her wish that money usually spent on gifts to pallbearers "should be given to the poor."

Anna Tuthill Symmes Harrison
1775-1864

Anna Harrison was too ill to travel when her husband set out from Ohio in 1841 for his inauguration. It was a long trip and a difficult one even by steamboat and railroad, with February weather uncertain at best, and she at age 65 was well acquainted with the rigors of frontier journeys.

As a girl of 19, bringing pretty clothes and dainty manners, she went out to Ohio with her father, Judge John Cleves Symmes, who had taken up land for settlement on the "north bend" of the Ohio River. She had grown up a young lady of the East, completing her education at a boarding school in New York City.

A clandestine marriage on November 25, 1795, united Anna Symmes and Lt. William Henry Harrison, an experienced soldier at 22. Though the young man came from one of the best families of Virginia, Judge Symmes did not want his daughter to face the hard life of frontier forts; but eventually, seeing her happiness, he accepted her choice.

Hostess for a single month: Jane Irwin Harrison, portrayed by an unknown artist.

Though Harrison won fame as an Indian fighter and hero of the War of 1812, he spent much of his life in a civilian career. His service in Congress as territorial delegate from Ohio gave Anna and their two children a chance to visit his family at Berkeley, their plantation on the James River. Her third child was born on that trip, at Richmond in September 1800. Harrison's appointment as governor of Indiana Territory took them even farther into the wilderness; he built a handsome house at Vincennes that blended fortress and plantation mansion. Five more children were born to Anna.

Facing war in 1812, the family went to the farm at North Bend. Before peace was assured, she had borne two more children. There, at news of her husband's landslide electoral victory in 1840, home-loving Anna said simply: "I wish that my husband's friends had left him where he is, happy and contented in retirement."

When she decided not to go to Washington with him, the President-elect asked his daughter-in-law Jane Irwin Harrison, widow of his namesake son, to accompany him and act as hostess until Anna's proposed arrival in May. Half a dozen other relatives happily went with them. On April 4, exactly one month after his inauguration, he died, so Anna never made the journey. She had already begun her packing when she learned of her loss.

Accepting grief with admirable dignity, she stayed at her home in North Bend until the house burned in 1858; she lived nearby with her last surviving child, John Scott Harrison, until she died in February 1864 at the age of 88.

Dressed in mourning, Anna Harrison posed for Cornelia Stuart Cassady in 1843—possibly at the Ohio home she had not left during her husband's Presidency. Her health precarious in 1841, she had temporarily entrusted the duties of White House hostess to her widowed daughter-in-law, Jane Irwin Harrison; before she could assume them herself, her husband died.

Heirloom portrait survived Civil War hazards to record the tranquil charm of Letitia Tyler for her descendants. An unknown artist painted it sometime before a paralytic stroke crippled her in 1839. At the White House she lived in seclusion. Her first daughter-in-law, Priscilla Cooper Tyler, assumed the duties of hostess until 1844, when she moved to Philadelphia. Between Letitia Tyler's death in 1842 and her husband's second marriage, the role of First Lady passed briefly to her second daughter, Letitia Tyler Semple.

Letitia Christian Tyler
1790-1842

Letitia Tyler had been confined to an invalid's chair for two years when her husband unexpectedly became President. Nobody had thought of that possibility when he took his oath of office as Vice President on March 4, 1841; indeed, he had planned to fill his undemanding duties from his home in Williamsburg where his wife was most comfortable, her Bible, prayer book, and knitting at her side.

Born on a Tidewater Virginia plantation in the 18th century, Letitia was spiritually akin to Martha Washington and Martha Jefferson. Formal education was no part of this pattern of life, but Letitia learned all the skills of managing a plantation, rearing a family, and presiding over a home that would be John Tyler's refuge during an active political life. They were married on March 29, 1813 — his twenty-third birthday. Thereafter, whether he served in Congress or as Governor of Virginia, she attended to domestic duties. Only once did she join him for the winter social season in Washington. Of the eight children she bore, seven survived; but after 1839 she was a cripple, though "still beautiful now in her declining years."

So her admiring new daughter-in-law, Priscilla Cooper Tyler, described her — "the most entirely unselfish person you can imagine. . . . Notwithstanding her very delicate health, mother attends to and regulates all the household affairs and all so quietly that you can't tell when she does it."

In a second-floor room at the White House, Letitia Tyler kept her quiet but pivotal role in family activities. She did not attempt to take part in the social affairs of the administration. Her married daughters had their own homes; the others were too young for the full responsibility of official entertaining; Priscilla at age 24 assumed the position of White House hostess, met its demands with spirit and success, and enjoyed it.

Daughter of a well-known tragedian, Priscilla Cooper had gone on the stage herself at 17. Playing Desdemona to her father's Othello in Richmond, she won the instant interest of Robert Tyler, whom she married in 1839. Intelligent and beautiful, with dark brown hair, she charmed the President's guests — from visiting celebrities like Charles Dickens to enthusiastic countrymen. Once she noted ruefully: "such hearty shakes as they gave my poor little hand too!" She enjoyed the expert advice of Dolley Madison, and the companionship of her young sister-in-law Elizabeth until she married William N. Waller in 1842.

For this wedding Letitia made her only appearance at a White House social function. "Lizzie looked surpassingly lovely," said Priscilla, and "our dear mother" was "far more attractive to me . . . than any other lady in the room," greeting her guests "in her sweet, gentle, self-possessed manner."

The first President's wife to die in the White House, Letitia Tyler ended her days peacefully on September 10, 1842, holding a damask rose in her hand. She was taken to Virginia for burial at the plantation of her birth, deeply mourned by her family. "She had everything about her," said Priscilla, "to awaken love. . . ."

Julia Gardiner Tyler
1820-1889

"I grieve my love a belle should be," sighed one of Julia Gardiner's innumerable admirers in 1840; at the age of 20 she was already famous as the "Rose of Long Island."

Daughter of Juliana McLachlan and David Gardiner, descendant of prominent and wealthy New York families, Julia was trained from earliest childhood for a life in society; she made her debut at 15. A European tour with her family gave her new glimpses of social splendors. Late in 1842 the Gardiners went to Washington for the winter social season, and Julia became the undisputed darling of the capital. Her beauty and her practiced charm attracted the most eminent men in the city, among them President Tyler, a widower since September.

Tragedy brought his courtship poignant success the next winter. Julia, her sister Margaret, and her father joined a Presidential excursion on the new steam frigate *Princeton;* and David Gardiner lost his life in the explosion of a huge naval gun. Tyler comforted Julia in her grief and won her consent to a secret engagement.

The first President to marry in office took his vows in New York on June 26, 1844. The news was then broken to the American people, who greeted it with keen interest, much publicity, and some criticism about the couple's difference in age: 30 years.

As young Mrs. Tyler said herself, she "reigned" as First Lady for the last eight months of her husband's term. Wearing white satin or black lace to obey the conventions of mourning, she presided with vivacity and animation at a series of parties. She enjoyed her position immensely, and filled it with grace. For receptions she revived the formality of the Van Buren administration; she welcomed her guests with plumes in her hair, attended by maids of honor dressed in white. She once declared, with truth: "Nothing appears to delight the President more than . . . to hear people sing my praises."

The Tylers' happiness was unshaken when they retired to their home at Sherwood Forest in Virginia. There Julia bore five of her seven children; and she acted as mistress of the plantation until the Civil War. As such, she defended both states' rights and the institution of slavery. She championed the political views of her husband, who remained for her "the President" until the end of his life.

His death in 1862 came as a severe blow to her. In a poem composed for his sixty-second birthday she had assured him that "what e'er changes time may bring, I'll love thee as thou art!"

Even as a refugee in New York, she devoted herself to volunteer work for the Confederacy. Its defeat found her impoverished. Not until 1958 would federal law provide automatic pensions for Presidential widows; but Congress in 1870 voted a pension for Mary Lincoln, and Julia Tyler used this precedent in seeking help. In December 1880 Congress voted her $1,200 a year—and after Garfield's assassination it passed bills to grant uniform amounts of $5,000 annually to Mrs. Garfield, Mrs. Lincoln, Mrs. Polk, and Mrs. Tyler. Living out her last years comfortably in Richmond, Julia died there in 1889 and was buried there at her husband's side.

"Most beautiful woman of the age and . . . most accomplished," President
Tyler called his new bride, who keenly enjoyed her success as hostess at
the White House. She posed for this portrait three years after leaving it.

"Time has dealt kindly with her personal charms. . . ," declared one of many admiring citizens when Sarah Polk became First Lady. In 1846 both she and her husband posed at the White House for George P. A. Healy; three years later they took his fine portraits home to "Polk Place" in Nashville, Tennessee. In her 80th year, ladies of the state commissioned a copy of hers for the Executive Mansion; they entrusted the work to George Dury, who had already painted her at 75 — still handsome and alert. Revered throughout the land, she kept her dignity of manner and her clarity of mind to the end.

Sarah Childress Polk
1803-1891

Silks and satins little Sarah took for granted, growing up on a plantation near Murfreesboro, Tennessee. Elder daughter of Captain Joel and Elizabeth Childress, she gained something rarer from her father's wealth. He sent her and her sister away to school, first to Nashville, then to the Moravians' "female academy" at Salem, North Carolina, one of the very few institutions of higher learning available to women in the early 19th century. So she acquired an education that made her especially fitted to assist a man with a political career.

James K. Polk was laying the foundation for that career when he met her. He had begun his first year's service in the Tennessee legislature when they were married on New Year's Day, 1824; he was 28, she 20. The story goes that Andrew Jackson had encouraged their romance; he certainly made Polk a political protégé, and as such Polk represented a district in Congress for 14 sessions.

In an age when motherhood gave a woman her only acknowledged career, Sarah Polk had to resign herself to childlessness. Moreover, no lady would admit to a political role of her own, but Mrs. Polk found scope for her astute mind as well as her social skills. She accompanied her husband to Washington whenever she could, and they soon won a place in its most select social circles. Constantly—but privately—Sarah was helping him with his speeches, copying his correspondence, giving him advice. Much as she enjoyed politics, she would warn him against overwork. He would hand her a newspaper—"Sarah, here is something I wish you to read. . . ."—and she would set to work as well.

A devout Presbyterian, she refused to attend horse races or the theater; but she always maintained social contacts of value to James. When he returned to Washington as President in 1845, she stepped to her high position with ease and evident pleasure. She appeared at the inaugural ball, but did not dance.

Contrasted with Julia Tyler's waltzes, her entertainments have become famous for sedateness and sobriety. Some later accounts say that the Polks never served wine, but in December 1845 a Congressman's wife recorded in her diary details of a four-hour dinner for forty at the White House—glasses for six different wines, from pink champagne to ruby port and sauterne, "formed a rainbow around each plate." Skilled in tactful conversation, Mrs. Polk enjoyed wide popularity as well as deep respect.

Only three months after retirement to their fine new home "Polk Place" in Nashville, he died, worn out by years of public service. Clad always in black, Sarah Polk lived on in that home for 42 years, guarding the memory of her husband and accepting honors paid to her as honors due to him. The house became a place of pilgrimage.

During the Civil War, Mrs. Polk held herself above sectional strife and received with dignity leaders of both Confederate and Union armies; all respected Polk Place as neutral ground. She presided over her house until her death in her 88th year. Buried beside her husband, she was mourned by a nation that had come to regard her as a precious link to the past.

Margaret Mackall Smith Taylor
1788-1852

After the election of 1848, a passenger on a Mississippi riverboat struck up a conversation with easy-mannered Gen. Zachary Taylor, not knowing his identity. The passenger remarked that he didn't think the general qualified for the Presidency—was the stranger "a Taylor man"? "Not much of a one," came the reply. The general went on to say that he hadn't voted for Taylor, partly because his wife was opposed to sending "Old Zack" to Washington, "where she would be obliged to go with him!" It was a truthful answer.

Moreover, the story goes that Margaret Taylor had taken a vow during the Mexican War: If her husband returned safely, she would never go into society again. In fact she never did, though prepared for it by genteel upbringing.

"Peggy" Smith was born in Calvert County, Maryland, daughter of Ann Mackall and Walter Smith, a major in the Revolutionary War according to family tradition. In 1809, visiting a sister in Kentucky, she met young Lieutenant Taylor. They were married the following June, and for a while the young wife stayed on the farm given them as a wedding present by Zachary's father. She bore her first baby there, but cheerfully followed her husband from one remote garrison to another along the western frontier of civilization. An admiring civilian official cited her as one of the "delicate females . . . reared in tenderness" who had to educate "worthy and most interesting" children at a fort in Indian country.

Two small girls died in 1820 of what Taylor called "a violent bilious fever," which left their mother's health impaired; three girls and a boy grew up. Knowing the hardships of a military wife, Taylor opposed his daughters' marrying career soldiers—but each eventually married into the Army.

The second daughter, Knox, married Lt. Jefferson Davis in gentle defiance of her parents. In a loving letter home, she imagined her mother skimming milk in the cellar or going out to feed the chickens. Within three months of her wedding, Knox died of malaria. Taylor was not reconciled to Davis until they fought together in Mexico; in Washington the second Mrs. Davis became a good friend of Mrs. Taylor's, often calling on her at the White House.

Though Peggy Taylor welcomed friends and kinfolk in her upstairs sitting room, presided at the family table, met special groups at her husband's side, and worshiped regularly at St. John's Episcopal Church, she took no part in formal social functions. She relegated all the duties of official hostess to her youngest daughter, Mary Elizabeth, then 25 and recent bride of Lt. Col. William W. S. Bliss, adjutant and secretary to the President. Betty Bliss filled her role admirably. One observer thought that her manner blended "the artlessness of a rustic belle and the grace of a duchess."

For Mrs. Taylor, her husband's death—on July 9, 1850—was an appalling blow. Never again did she speak of the White House. She spent her last days with the Blisses, dying on August 18, 1852.

Hostess in her mother's stead, Betty Taylor Bliss probably posed for this daguerreotype about a decade after her White House days. Of Mrs. Taylor, a semi-invalid for years, no authentic likeness survives; contemporaries described her as slender and stately, a brunette in youth.

Abigail Powers Fillmore
1798-1853

First of First Ladies to hold a job after marriage, Abigail Fillmore was helping her husband's career. She was also revealing her most striking personal characteristic: eagerness to learn and pleasure in teaching others.

She was born in Saratoga County, New York, in 1798, while it was still on the fringe of civilization. Her father, a locally prominent Baptist preacher named Lemuel Powers, died shortly thereafter. Courageously, her mother moved on westward, thinking her scanty funds would go further in a less settled region, and ably educated her small son and daughter beyond the usual frontier level with the help of her husband's library.

Shared eagerness for schooling formed a bond when Abigail Powers at 21 met Millard Fillmore at 19, both students at a recently opened academy in the village of New Hope. Although she soon became young Fillmore's inspiration, his struggle to make his way as a lawyer was so long and ill paid that they were not married until February 1826. She even resumed teaching school after the marriage. And then her only son, Millard Powers, was born in 1828.

Attaining prosperity at last, Fillmore bought his family a six-room house in Buffalo, where little Mary Abigail was born in 1832. Enjoying comparative luxury, Abigail learned the ways of society as the wife of a Congressman. She cultivated a noted flower garden; but much of her time, as always, she spent in reading. In 1847, Fillmore was elected state comptroller; with the children away in boarding school and college, the parents moved temporarily to Albany.

In 1849, Abigail Fillmore came to Washington as wife of the Vice President; 16 months later, after Zachary Taylor's death at a height of sectional crisis, the Fillmores moved into the White House.

Even after the period of official mourning the social life of the Fillmore administration remained subdued. The First Lady presided with grace at state dinners and receptions; but a permanently injured ankle made her Friday-evening levees an ordeal—two hours of standing at her husband's side to greet the public. In any case, she preferred reading or music in private. Pleading her delicate health, she entrusted many routine social duties to her attractive daughter, "Abby." With a special appropriation from Congress, she spent contented hours selecting books for a White House library and arranging them in the oval room upstairs, where Abby had her piano, harp, and guitar. Here, wrote a friend, Mrs. Fillmore "could enjoy the music she so much loved, and the conversation of . . . cultivated society. . . ."

Despite chronic poor health, Mrs. Fillmore stayed near her husband through the outdoor ceremonies of President Pierce's inauguration while a raw northeast wind whipped snow over the crowd. Returning chilled to the Willard Hotel, she developed pneumonia; she died there on March 30, 1853. The House of Representatives and the Senate adjourned, and public offices closed in respect, as her family took her body home to Buffalo for burial.

Maternal dignity of a matron in middle life dominates this likeness of Abigail Fillmore record-ed by a daguerreotype. By contemporary descriptions Mrs. Fillmore had been fair of coloring and taller at 5 feet 6 inches than the average woman of her time. A snippet of Washington gossip suggests her manner as First Lady, accusing her of lacking "good form" in seeming "so motherly to her guests." In the duties of hostess her daughter Mary Abigail gave her wel-come help. "Abby," a talented young woman of poise and polish, managed the former Presi-dent's household from her mother's death until her own shockingly unexpected death at age 22. Fillmore found escape from loneliness in a second happy marriage: to Caroline Carmichael McIntosh, a wealthy and childless widow who survived him.

Jane Means Appleton Pierce
1806-1863

In looks and in pathetic destiny young Jane Means Appleton resembled the heroine of a Victorian novel. The gentle dignity of her face reflected her sensitive, retiring personality and physical weakness. Her father had died—he was a Congregational minister, the Reverend Jesse Appleton, president of Bowdoin College—and her mother had taken the family to Amherst, New Hampshire. And Jane met a Bowdoin graduate, a young lawyer with political ambitions, Franklin Pierce.

Although he was immediately devoted to Jane, they did not marry until she was 28—surprising in that day of early marriages. Her family opposed the match; moreover, she always did her best to discourage his interest in politics. The death of a three-day-old son, the arrival of a new baby, and Jane's dislike of Washington counted heavily in his decision to retire at the apparent height of his career, as United States Senator, in 1842. Little Frank Robert, the second son, died the next year of typhus.

Service in the Mexican War brought Pierce the rank of brigadier and local fame as a hero. He returned home safely, and for four years the Pierces lived quietly at Concord, New Hampshire, in the happiest period of their lives. With attentive pleasure Jane watched her son Benjamin growing up.

Then, in 1852, the Democratic Party made Pierce their candidate for President. His wife fainted at the news. When he took her to Newport for a respite, Benny wrote to her: "I hope he won't be elected for I should not like to be at Washington and I know you would not either." But the President-elect convinced Jane that his office would be an asset for Benny's success in life.

On a journey by train, January 6, 1853, their car was derailed and Benny killed before their eyes. The whole nation shared the parents' grief. The inauguration on March 4 took place without an inaugural ball and without the presence of Mrs. Pierce. She joined her husband later that month, but any pleasure the White House might have brought her was gone. From this loss she never recovered fully. Other events deepened the somber mood of the new administration: Mrs. Fillmore's death in March, that of Vice President Rufus King in April.

Always devout, Jane Pierce turned for solace to prayer. She had to force herself to meet the social obligations inherent in the role of First Lady. Fortunately she had the companionship and help of a girlhood friend, now her aunt by marriage, Abigail Kent Means. Mrs. Robert E. Lee wrote in a private letter: "I have known many of the ladies of the White House, none more truly excellent than the afflicted wife of President Pierce. Her health was a bar to any great effort on her part to meet the expectations of the public in her high position but she was a refined, extremely religious and well educated lady."

With retirement, the Pierces made a prolonged trip abroad in search of health for the invalid—she carried Benny's Bible throughout the journey. The quest was unsuccessful, so the couple came home to New Hampshire to be near family and friends until Jane's death in 1863. She was buried near Benny's grave.

*Treasure for a family's annals, this likeness — a photograph from about 1850
— captures the mutual devotion of Jane Pierce and Benny, last of her three
sons. Two months before Pierce's inauguration, a railroad accident killed
11-year-old Benny before his parents' eyes. When his stricken mother
finally brought herself to appear at White House functions, the guests who
acknowledged her "winning smile" could not fail to recognize the "traces
of bereavement . . . on a countenance too ingenuous for concealment. . . ."*

Harriet Lane
1830-1903

Unique among First Ladies, Harriet Lane acted as hostess for the only President who never married: James Buchanan, her favorite uncle and her guardian after she was orphaned at the age of eleven. And of all the ladies of the White House, few achieved such great success in deeply troubled times as this polished young woman in her twenties.

In the rich farming country of Franklin County, Pennsylvania, her family had prospered as merchants. Her uncle supervised her sound education in private school, completed by two years at the Visitation Convent in Georgetown. By this time "Nunc" was Secretary of State, and he introduced her to fashionable circles as he had promised, "in the best manner." In 1854 she joined him in London, where he was minister to the Court of St. James's. Queen Victoria gave "dear Miss Lane" the rank of ambassador's wife; admiring suitors gave her the fame of a beauty.

In appearance "Hal" Lane was of medium height, with masses of light hair almost golden. In manner she enlivened social gatherings with a captivating mixture of spontaneity and poise.

After the sadness of the Pierce administration, the capital eagerly welcomed its new "Democratic Queen" in 1857. Harriet Lane filled the White House with gaiety and flowers, and guided its social life with enthusiasm and discretion, winning national popularity.

As sectional tensions increased, she worked out seating arrangements for her weekly formal dinner parties with special care, to give dignitaries their proper precedence and still keep political foes apart. Her tact did not falter, but her task became impossible—as did her uncle's. Seven states had seceded by the time Buchanan retired from office and thankfully returned with his niece to his spacious country home, Wheatland, near Lancaster, Pennsylvania.

From her teenage years, the popular Miss Lane flirted happily with numerous beaux, calling them "pleasant but dreadfully troublesome." Buchanan often warned her against "rushing precipitately into matrimonial connexions," and she waited until she was almost 36 to marry. She chose, with her uncle's approval, Henry Elliott Johnston, a Baltimore banker. Within the next 18 years she faced one sorrow after another: the loss of her uncle, her two fine young sons, and her husband.

Thereafter she decided to live in Washington, among friends made during years of happiness. She had acquired a sizable art collection, largely of European works, which she bequeathed to the government. Accepted after her death in 1903, it inspired an official of the Smithsonian Institution to call her "First Lady of the National Collection of Fine Arts." In addition, she had dedicated a generous sum to endow a home for invalid children at the Johns Hopkins Hospital in Baltimore. It became an outstanding pediatric facility, and its national reputation is a fitting memorial to the young lady who presided at the White House with such dignity and charm. The Harriet Lane Outpatient Clinics serve thousands of children today.

"Mischievous romp of a niece," James Buchanan once called the little tomboy who at age 26 became White House hostess for the bachelor President. Artist John Henry Brown captured her queenly beauty 21 years after Harriet Lane assumed the role of First Lady. Fun-loving and flirtatious, spending lavishly on parties and clothes, she brightened a gloomy administration as civil war threatened it, warning her guests to refrain from political discussions.

Mary Todd Lincoln
1818-1882

As a girlhood companion remembered her, Mary Todd was vivacious and impulsive, with an interesting personality—but "she now and then could not restrain a witty, sarcastic speech that cut deeper than she intended. . . ." A young lawyer summed her up in 1840: "the very creature of excitement." All of these attributes marked her life, bringing her both happiness and tragedy.

Daughter of Eliza Parker and Robert Smith Todd, pioneer settlers of Kentucky, Mary lost her mother before the age of seven. Her father remarried; and Mary remembered her childhood as "desolate" although she belonged to the aristocracy of Lexington, with high-spirited social life and a sound private education.

Just 5 feet 2 inches at maturity, Mary had clear blue eyes, long lashes, light-brown hair with glints of bronze, and a lovely complexion. She danced gracefully, she loved finery, and her crisp intelligence polished the wiles of a Southern coquette.

Nearly 21, she went to Springfield, Illinois, to live with her sister Mrs. Ninian Edwards. Here she met Abraham Lincoln—in his own words, "a poor nobody then." Three years later, after a stormy courtship and broken engagement, they were married. Though opposites in background and temperament, they were united by an enduring love—by Mary's confidence in her husband's ability and his gentle consideration of her excitable ways.

Their years in Springfield brought hard work, a family of boys, and reduced circumstances to the pleasure-loving girl who had never felt responsibility before. Lincoln's single term in Congress, for 1847-1849, gave Mary and the boys a winter in Washington, but scant opportunity for social life. Finally her unwavering faith in her husband won ample justification with his election as President in 1860.

Though her position fulfilled her high social ambitions, Mrs. Lincoln's years in the White House mingled misery with triumph. An orgy of spending stirred resentful comment. While the Civil War dragged on, Southerners scorned her as a traitor to her birth, and citizens loyal to the Union suspected her of treason. When she entertained, critics accused her of unpatriotic extravagance. When, utterly distraught, she curtailed her entertaining after her son Willie's death in 1862, they accused her of shirking her social duties.

Yet Lincoln, watching her put her guests at ease during a White House reception, could say happily: "My wife is as handsome as when she was a girl, and I . . . fell in love with her; and what is more, I have never fallen out."

Her husband's assassination in 1865 shattered Mary Todd Lincoln. The next 17 years held nothing but sorrow. With her son "Tad" she traveled abroad in search of health, tortured by distorted ideas of her financial situation. After Tad died in 1871, she slipped into a world of illusion where poverty and murder pursued her.

A misunderstood and tragic figure, she passed away in 1882 at her sister's home in Springfield—the same house from which she had walked as the bride of Abraham Lincoln, 40 years before.

Mathew Brady's camera reveals Mary Lincoln before hostile gossip, private grief, and national tragedy had marked her face—probably in 1861. Of six portraits he made that year, she found only a profile "passable."

Married at 16, Eliza McCardle Johnson taught her husband writing and arithmetic. In poor health when she went to the White House, she left the duties of First Lady to her daughter Martha Patterson (opposite), who modestly said of her family: "We are plain people, from the mountains of Tennessee, called here for a short time by a national calamity. I trust too much will not be expected of us." Byrd Venable Farioletti painted Mrs. Johnson's portrait in 1961, from a photograph taken during the White House years.

Eliza McCardle Johnson
1810-1876

"I knew he'd be acquitted; I knew it," declared Eliza McCardle Johnson, told how the Senate had voted in her husband's impeachment trial. Her faith in him had never wavered during those difficult days in 1868, when her courage dictated that all White House social events should continue as usual.

That faith began to develop many years before in east Tennessee, when Andrew Johnson first came to Greeneville, across the mountains from North Carolina, and established a tailor shop. Eliza was almost 16 then and Andrew only 17; and local tradition tells of the day she first saw him. He was driving a blind pony hitched to a small cart, and she said to a girl friend, "There goes my beau!" She married him within a year, on May 17, 1827.

Eliza was the daughter of Sarah Phillips and John McCardle, a shoemaker. Fortunately she had received a good basic education that she was delighted to share with her new husband. He already knew his letters and could read a bit, so she taught him writing and arithmetic. With their limited means, her skill at keeping a house and bringing up a family—five children, in all— had much to do with Johnson's success.

Martha Johnson Patterson, wearing onyx earrings that Mrs. Polk had given to her.

He rose rapidly, serving in the state and national legislatures and as governor. Like him, when the Civil War came, people of east Tennessee remained loyal to the Union; Lincoln sent him to Nashville as military governor in 1862. Rebel forces caught Eliza at home with part of the family. Only after months of uncertainty did they rejoin Andrew Johnson in Nashville. By 1865 a soldier son and son-in-law had died, and Eliza was an invalid for life.

Quite aside from the tragedy of Lincoln's death, she found little pleasure in her husband's position as President. At the White House, she settled into a second-floor room that became the center of activities for a large family: her two sons, her widowed daughter Mary Stover and her children; her older daughter Martha with her husband, Senator David T. Patterson, and their children. As a schoolgirl Martha had often been the Polks' guest at the mansion; now she took up its social duties. She was a competent, unpretentious, and gracious hostess even during the impeachment crisis.

At the end of Johnson's term, Eliza returned with relief to her home in Tennessee, restored from wartime vandalism. She lived to see the legislature of her state vindicate her husband's career by electing him to the Senate in 1875, and survived him by nearly six months, dying at the Pattersons' home in 1876.

Julia Dent Grant
1826-1902

Quite naturally, shy young Lieutenant Grant lost his heart to friendly Julia; and he made his love known, as he said himself years later, "in the most awkward manner imaginable." She told her side of the story—her father opposed the match, saying, "the boy is too poor," and she answered angrily that she was poor herself. The "poverty" on her part came from a slave-owner's lack of ready cash.

Daughter of Frederick and Ellen Wrenshall Dent, Julia had grown up on a plantation near St. Louis in a typically Southern atmosphere. In memoirs prepared late in life—unpublished until 1975—she pictured her girlhood as an idyll: "one long summer of sunshine, flowers, and smiles. . . ." She attended the Misses Mauros' boarding school in St. Louis for seven years among the daughters of other affluent parents. A social favorite in that circle, she met "Ulys" at her home, where her family welcomed him as a West Point classmate of her brother Frederick; soon she felt lonely without him, dreamed of him, and agreed to wear his West Point ring.

Julia and her handsome lieutenant became engaged in 1844, but the Mexican War deferred the wedding for four long years. Their marriage, often tried by adversity, met every test; they gave each other a life-long loyalty. Like other army wives, "dearest Julia" accompanied her husband to military posts, to pass uneventful days at distant garrisons. Then she returned to his parents' home in 1852 when he was ordered to the West.

Ending that separation, Grant resigned his commission two years later. Farming and business ventures at St. Louis failed, and in 1860 he took his family—four children now—back to his home in Galena, Illinois. He was working in his father's leather goods store when the Civil War called him to a soldier's duty with his state's volunteers. Throughout the war, Julia joined her husband near the scene of action whenever she could.

After so many years of hardship and stress, she rejoiced in his fame as a victorious general, and she entered the White House in 1869 to begin, in her words, "the happiest period" of her life. With Cabinet wives as her allies, she entertained extensively and lavishly. Contemporaries noted her finery, jewels and silks and laces.

Upon leaving the White House in 1877, the Grants made a trip around the world that became a journey of triumphs. Julia proudly recalled details of hospitality and magnificent gifts they received.

But in 1884 Grant suffered yet another business failure and they lost all they had. To provide for his wife, Grant wrote his famous personal memoirs, racing with time and death from cancer. The means thus afforded and her widow's pension enabled her to live in comfort, surrounded by children and grandchildren, till her own death in 1902. She had attended in 1897 the dedication of Grant's monumental tomb in New York City where she was laid to rest. She had ended her own chronicle of their years together with a firm declaration: "the light of his glorious fame still reaches out to me, falls upon me, and warms me."

At Mathew Brady's studio, Julia Dent Grant adopts a characteristic pose to hide an eye defect. Grant rejected the idea of corrective surgery, teasing her gently: ''...I might not like you half so well with any other eyes.''

Lucy Ware Webb Hayes
1831-1889

There was no inaugural ball in 1877 — when Rutherford B. Hayes and his wife, Lucy, left Ohio for Washington, the outcome of the election was still in doubt. Public fears had not subsided when it was settled in Hayes' favor; and when Lucy watched her husband take his oath of office at the Capitol, her serene and beautiful face impressed even cynical journalists.

She came to the White House well loved by many. Born in Chillicothe, Ohio, daughter of Maria Cook and Dr. James Webb, she lost her father at age two. She was just entering her teens when Mrs. Webb took her sons to the town of Delaware to enroll in the new Ohio Wesleyan University, but she began studying with its excellent instructors. She graduated from the Wesleyan Female College in Cincinnati at 18, unusually well educated for a young lady of her day.

"Rud" Hayes at 27 had set up a law practice in Cincinnati, and he began paying calls at the Webb home. References to Lucy appeared in his diary: "Her low sweet voice is very winning...a heart as true as steel.... Intellect she has too.... By George! I am in love with her!" Married in 1852, they lived in Cincinnati until the Civil War, and he soon came to share her deeply religious opposition to slavery. Visits to relatives and vacation journeys broke the routine of a happy domestic life in a growing family. Over twenty years Lucy bore eight children, of whom five grew up.

She won the affectionate name of "Mother Lucy" from men of the 23rd Ohio Volunteer Infantry who served under her husband's command in the war. They remembered her visits to camp — to minister to the wounded, cheer the homesick, and comfort the dying. Hayes' distinguished combat record earned him election to Congress, and three postwar terms as governor of Ohio. She not only joined him in Washington for its winter social season, she also accompanied him on visits to state reform schools, prisons, and asylums. As the popular first lady of her state, she gained experience in what a woman of her time aptly called "semi-public life."

Thus she entered the White House with confidence gained from her long and happy married life, her knowledge of political circles, her intelligence and culture, and her cheerful spirit. She enjoyed informal parties, and spared no effort to make official entertaining attractive. Though she was a temperance advocate and liquor was banned at the mansion during this administration, she was a very popular hostess. She took criticism of her views in good humor (the famous nickname "Lemonade Lucy" apparently came into use only after she had left the mansion). She became one of the best-loved women to preside over the White House, where the Hayeses celebrated their silver wedding anniversary in 1877, and an admirer hailed her as representing "the new woman era."

The Hayes term ended in 1881, and the family home was now "Spiegel Grove," an estate at Fremont, Ohio. There husband and wife spent eight active, contented years together until her death in 1889. She was buried in Fremont, mourned by her family and hosts of friends.

Sunny in temperament, winning in manner, firm in high principle, Lucy Hayes met both praise and gibes when White House menus omitted liquor. The Woman's Christian Temperance Union honored her with this portrait.

Intellectual Lucretia Garfield—"Crete" to the husband who depended upon her political insights—may have posed for this Brady study while still a Congressman's wife. Illness and turmoil filled her 200 days as First Lady.

Lucretia Rudolph Garfield
1832-1918

In the fond eyes of her husband, President James A. Garfield, Lucretia "grows up to every new emergency with fine tact and faultless taste." She proved this in the eyes of the nation, though she was always a reserved, self-contained woman. She flatly refused to pose for a campaign photograph, and much preferred a literary circle or informal party to a state reception.

Her love of learning she acquired from her father, Zeb Rudolph, a leading citizen of Hiram, Ohio, and devout member of the Disciples of Christ. She first met "Jim" Garfield when both attended a nearby school, and they renewed their friendship in 1851 as students at the Western Reserve Eclectic Institute, founded by the Disciples.

But "Crete" did not attract his special attention until December 1853, when he began a rather cautious courtship, and they did not marry until November 1858, when he was well launched on his career as a teacher. His service in the Union Army from 1861 to 1863 kept them apart; their first child, a daughter, died in 1863. But after his first lonely winter in Washington as a freshman Representative, the family remained together. With a home in the capital as well as one in Ohio they enjoyed a happy domestic life. A two-year-old son died in 1876, but five children grew up healthy and promising; with the passage of time, Lucretia became more and more her husband's companion.

In Washington they shared intellectual interests with congenial friends; she went with him to meetings of a locally celebrated literary society. They read together, made social calls together, dined with each other and traveled in company until by 1880 they were as nearly inseparable as his career permitted.

Garfield's election to the Presidency brought a cheerful family to the White House in 1881. Though Mrs. Garfield was not particularly interested in a First Lady's social duties, she was deeply conscientious and her genuine hospitality made her dinners and twice-weekly receptions enjoyable. At the age of 49 she was still a slender, graceful little woman with clear dark eyes, her brown hair beginning to show traces of silver.

In May she fell gravely ill, apparently from malaria and nervous exhaustion, to her husband's profound distress. "When you are sick," he had written her seven years earlier, "I am like the inhabitants of countries visited by earthquakes." She was still a convalescent, at a seaside resort in New Jersey, when he was shot by a demented assassin on July 2. She returned to Washington by special train—"frail, fatigued, desperate," reported an eyewitness at the White House, "but firm and quiet and full of purpose to save."

During the three months her husband fought for his life, her grief, devotion, and fortitude won the respect and sympathy of the country. In September, after his death, the bereaved family went home to their farm in Ohio. For another 36 years she led a strictly private but busy and comfortable life, active in preserving the records of her husband's career. She died on March 14, 1918.

Daily throughout his White House years, according to family tradition, President Chester A. Arthur had a fresh bouquet of flowers placed before this hand-tinted, silver-framed photograph of his wife. Ellen Herndon Arthur had died ten months before his election to the Vice Presidency. A sophisticated host in his own right, he asked his sister Mary McElroy to assume the role of White House hostess for form's sake, and to oversee the care of his motherless daughter, Ellen.

Ellen Lewis Herndon Arthur
1837-1880

Chester Alan Arthur's beloved "Nell" died of pneumonia on January 12, 1880. That November, when he was elected Vice President, he was still mourning her bitterly. In his own words: "Honors to me now are not what they once were." His grief was the more poignant because she was only 42 and her death sudden. Just two days earlier she had attended a benefit concert in New York City — while he was busy with politics in Albany — and she caught cold that night while waiting for her carriage. She was already unconscious when he reached her side.

Her family connections among distinguished Virginians had shaped her life. She was born at Culpeper Court House, only child of Elizabeth Hansbrough and William Lewis Herndon, U.S.N. They moved to Washington, D. C., when he was assigned to help his brother-in-law Lt. Matthew Fontaine Maury establish the Naval Observatory. While Ellen was still just a girl her beautiful contralto voice attracted attention; she joined the choir at St. John's Episcopal Church on Lafayette Square.

Then her father assumed command of a mail steamer operating from New York; and in 1856 a cousin introduced her to "Chet" Arthur, who was establishing a law practice in the city. By 1857 they were engaged. In a birthday letter that year he reminded her of "the soft, moonlight nights of June, a year ago ... happy, happy days at Saratoga — the golden, fleeting hours at Lake George." He wished he could hear her singing.

That same year her father died a hero's death at sea, going down with his ship in a gale off Cape Hatteras. The marriage did not take place until October 1859; and a son named for Commander Herndon died when only two. But another boy was born in

Mary Arthur McElroy: youngest sister of the President, ranking lady of the Arthur administration.

1864 and a girl, named for her mother, in 1871. Arthur's career brought the family an increasing prosperity; they decorated their home in the latest fashion and entertained prominent friends with elegance. At Christmas there were jewels from Tiffany for Nell, the finest toys for the children.

At the White House, Arthur would not give anyone the place that would have been his wife's. He asked his sister Mary (Mrs. John E. McElroy) to assume certain social duties and help care for his daughter. He presented a stained-glass window to St. John's Church in his wife's memory; it depicted angels of the Resurrection, and at his special request it was placed in the south transept so that he could see it at night from the White House with the lights of the church shining through.

Frances Folsom Cleveland
1864-1947

"I detest him so much that I don't even think his wife is beautiful." So spoke one of President Grover Cleveland's political foes — the only person, it seems, to deny the loveliness of this notable First Lady, first bride of a President to be married in the White House.

She was born in Buffalo, New York, only child of Emma C. Harmon and Oscar Folsom — who became a law partner of Cleveland's. As a devoted family friend Cleveland bought "Frank" her first baby carriage. As administrator of the Folsom

Rose Elizabeth Cleveland: her bachelor brother's hostess in 15 months of his first term of office.

estate after his partner's death, though never her legal guardian, he guided her education with sound advice. When she entered Wells College, he asked Mrs. Folsom's permission to correspond with her, and he kept her room bright with flowers.

Though Frank and her mother missed his inauguration in 1885, they visited him at the White House that spring. There affection turned into romance — despite 27 years' difference in age — and there the wedding took place on June 2, 1886.

Cleveland's scholarly sister Rose gladly gave up the duties of hostess for her own career in education; and with a bride as First Lady, state entertainments took on a new interest. Mrs. Cleveland's unaffected charm won her immediate popularity. She held two receptions a week — one on Saturday afternoons, when women with jobs were free to come.

After the President's defeat in 1888, the Clevelands lived in New York City, where baby Ruth was born. With his unprecedented re-election, the First Lady returned to the White House as if she had been gone but a day. Through the political storms of this term she always kept her place in public favor. People took keen interest in the birth of Esther at the mansion in 1893, and of Marion in 1895. When the family left the White House, Mrs. Cleveland had become one of the most popular women ever to serve as hostess for the nation.

She bore two sons while the Clevelands lived in Princeton, New Jersey, and was at her husband's side when he died at their home, "Westland," in 1908.

In 1913 she married Thomas J. Preston, Jr., a professor of archeology, and remained a figure of note in the Princeton community until she died. She had reached her 84th year — nearly the age at which the venerable Mrs. Polk had welcomed her and her husband on a Presidential visit to the South, and chatted of changes in White House life from bygone days.

Youngest of First Ladies, Frances Folsom Cleveland stirred the public's sentimental admiration as a White House bride at 21 and earned nation-wide respect as a charming hostess, a loyal wife, and a capable mother. As President Cleveland expected, she proved "pretty level-headed." The fashion-able Swedish portraitist Anders L. Zorn painted this study from life in 1899.

Caroline Lavinia Scott Harrison
1832-1892

The centennial of President Washington's inauguration heightened the nation's interest in its heroic past, and in 1890 Caroline Scott Harrison lent her prestige as First Lady to the founding of the National Society of the Daughters of the American Revolution. She served as its first President General. She took a special interest in the history of the White House, and the mature dignity with which she carried out her duties may overshadow the fun-loving nature that had charmed "Ben" Harrison when they met as teenagers.

Born at Oxford, Ohio, in 1832, "Carrie" was the second daughter of Mary Potts Neal and the Reverend Dr. John W. Scott, a Presbyterian minister and founder of the Oxford Female Institute. As her father's pupil—brown-haired, petite, witty—she infatuated the reserved young Ben, then an honor student at Miami University; they were engaged before his graduation and married in 1853.

After early years of struggle while he established a law practice in Indianapolis, they enjoyed a happy family life interrupted only by the Civil War. Then, while General Harrison became a man of note in his profession, his wife cared for their son and daughter, gave active service to the First Presbyterian Church and to an orphans' home, and extended cordial hospitality to her many friends. Church views to the contrary, she saw no harm in private dancing lessons for her daughter—she liked dancing herself. Blessed with considerable artistic talent, she was an accomplished pianist; she especially enjoyed painting for recreation.

Illness repeatedly kept her away from Washington's winter social season during her husband's term in the Senate, 1881-1887, and she welcomed their return to private life; but she moved with poise to the White House in 1889 to continue the gracious way of life she had always created in her own home.

During the administration the Harrisons' daughter, Mary Harrison McKee, her two children, and other relatives lived at the White House. The First Lady tried in vain to have the overcrowded mansion enlarged but managed to assure an extensive renovation with up-to-date improvements. She established the collection of china associated with White House history. She worked for local charities as well. With other ladies of progressive views, she helped raise funds for the Johns Hopkins University medical school on condition that it admit women. She gave elegant receptions and dinners. In the winter of 1891-1892, however, she had to battle illness as she tried to fulfill her social obligations. She died of tuberculosis at the White House in October 1892, and after services in the East Room was buried from her own church in Indianapolis.

When official mourning ended, Mrs. McKee acted as hostess for her father in the last months of his term. (In 1896 he married his first wife's widowed niece and former secretary, Mary Scott Lord Dimmick; she survived him by nearly 47 years, dying in January 1948.)

To honor the memory of their first President General, Caroline Harrison, the Daughters of the American Revolution commissioned this posthumous portrait by Daniel Huntington and presented it to the White House in 1894.

Ida Saxton McKinley
1847-1907

There was little resemblance between the vivacious young woman who married William McKinley in January 1871 — a slender bride with sky-blue eyes and fair skin and masses of auburn hair — and the petulant invalid who moved into the White House with him in March 1897. Now her face was pallid and drawn, her close-cropped hair gray; her eyes were glazed with pain or dulled with sedative. Only one thing had remained the same: love which had brightened early years of happiness and endured through more than twenty years of illness.

Ida had been born in Canton, Ohio, in 1847, elder daughter of a socially prominent and well-to-do family. James A. Saxton, a banker, was indulgent to his two daughters. He educated them well in local schools and a finishing school, and then sent them to Europe on the grand tour.

Being pretty, fashionable, and a leader of the younger set in Canton did not satisfy Ida, so her broad-minded father suggested that she work in his bank. As a cashier she caught the attention of Maj. William McKinley, who had come to Canton in 1867 to establish a law practice, and they fell deeply in love. While he advanced in his profession, his young wife devoted her time to home and husband. A daughter, Katherine, was born on Christmas Day, 1871; a second, in April 1873. This time Ida was seriously ill, and the frail baby died in August. Phlebitis and epileptic seizures shattered the mother's health; and even before little Katie died in 1876, she was a confirmed invalid.

As Congressman and then as governor of Ohio, William McKinley was never far from her side. He arranged their life to suit her convenience. She spent most of her waking hours in a small Victorian rocking chair that she had had since childhood; she sat doing fancywork and crocheting bedroom slippers while she waited for her husband, who indulged her every whim.

At the White House, the McKinleys acted as if her health were no great handicap to her role as First Lady. Richly and prettily dressed, she received guests at formal receptions seated in a blue velvet chair. She held a fragrant bouquet to suggest that she would not shake hands. Contrary to protocol, she was seated beside the President at state dinners and he, as always, kept close watch for signs of an impending seizure. If necessary, he would cover her face with a large handkerchief for a moment. The First Lady and her devoted husband seemed oblivious to any social inadequacy. Guests were discreet and newspapers silent on the subject of her "fainting spells." Only in recent years have the facts of her health been revealed.

When the President was shot by an assassin in September 1901, after his second inauguration, he thought primarily of her. He murmured to his secretary: "My wife — be careful, Cortelyou, how you tell her — oh, be careful." After his death she lived in Canton, cared for by her younger sister, visiting her husband's grave almost daily. She died in 1907, and lies entombed beside the President and near their two little daughters in Canton's McKinley Memorial Mausoleum.

Both Ida McKinley and her devoted husband posed in the private quarters of the White House for watercolor miniatures by Emily Drayton Taylor in April 1899. Despite varied illnesses, including epilepsy, she took up the role of First Lady with an indomitable determination.

With assured, cultivated taste, Edith Roosevelt approved decor for a renovated White House in 1902; she decided that the new ground-floor corridor, entryway for guests on important occasions, should display likenesses of "all the ladies . . . including myself." That same year Theobald Chartran had painted her confidently posed in the South Grounds. Her firmness and prudent advice earned the deep respect of her exuberant husband, and all who knew her. Ever since her day, the corridor has served as a gallery for portraits of recent First Ladies.

Edith Kermit Carow Roosevelt
1861-1948

Edith Kermit Carow knew Theodore Roosevelt from infancy; as a toddler she became a playmate of his younger sister Corinne. Born in Connecticut in 1861, daughter of Charles and Gertrude Tyler Carow, she grew up in an old New York brownstone on Union Square—an environment of comfort and tradition. Throughout childhood she and "Teedie" were in and out of each other's houses.

Attending Miss Comstock's school, she acquired the proper finishing touch for a young lady of that era. A quiet girl who loved books, she was often Theodore's companion for summer outings at Oyster Bay, Long Island; but this ended when he entered Harvard. Although she attended his wedding to Alice Hathaway Lee in 1880, their lives ran separately until 1885, when he was a young widower with an infant daughter, Alice.

Putting tragedy behind him, he and Edith were married in London in December 1886. They settled down in a house on Sagamore Hill, at Oyster Bay, headquarters for a family that added five children in ten years: Theodore, Kermit, Ethel, Archibald, and Quentin. Throughout Roosevelt's intensely active career, family life remained close and entirely delightful. A small son remarked one day, "When Mother was a little girl, she must have been a boy!"

Public tragedy brought them into the White House, eleven days after President McKinley succumbed to an assassin's bullet. Assuming her new duties with characteristic dignity, Mrs. Roosevelt meant to guard the privacy of a family that attracted everyone's interest, and she tried to keep reporters outside her domain. The public, in consequence, heard little of the vigor of her character, her sound judgment, her efficient household management.

But in this administration the White House was unmistakably the social center of the land. Beyond the formal occasions, smaller parties brought together distinguished men and women from varied walks of life. Two family events were highlights: the wedding of "Princess Alice" to Nicholas Longworth, and Ethel's debut. A perceptive aide described the First Lady as "always the gentle, high-bred hostess; smiling often at what went on about her, yet never critical of the ignorant and tolerant always of the little insincerities of political life."

T.R. once wrote to Ted Jr. that "if Mother had been a mere unhealthy Patient Griselda I might have grown set in selfish and inconsiderate ways." She continued, with keen humor and unfailing dignity, to balance her husband's exuberance after they retired in 1909.

After his death in 1919, she traveled widely abroad but always returned to Sagamore Hill as her home. Alone much of the time, she never appeared lonely, being still an avid reader—"not only cultured but scholarly," as T.R. had said. She kept till the end her interest in the Needlework Guild, a charity which provided garments for the poor, and in the work of Christ Church at Oyster Bay. She died on September 30, 1948, at the age of 87.

Helen Herron Taft
1861-1943

As "the only unusual incident" of her girlhood, "Nellie" Herron Taft recalled her visit to the White House at 17 as the guest of President and Mrs. Hayes, intimate friends of her parents. Fourth child of Harriet Collins and John W. Herron, born in 1861, she had grown up in Cincinnati, Ohio, attending a private school in the city and studying music with enthusiasm.

The year after this notable visit she met "that adorable Will Taft," a tall young lawyer, at a sledding party. They found intellectual interests in common; friendship matured into love; Helen Herron and William Howard Taft were married in 1886. A "treasure," he called her, "self-contained, independent, and of unusual application." He wondered if they would ever reach Washington "in any official capacity" and suggested to her that they might—when she became Secretary of the Treasury!

No woman could hope for such a career in that day, but Mrs. Taft welcomed each step in her husband's: state judge, Solicitor General of the United States, federal circuit judge. In 1900 he agreed to take charge of American civil government in the Philippines. By now the children numbered three: Robert, Helen, and Charles. The delight with which she undertook the journey, and her willingness to take her children to a country still unsettled by war, were characteristic of this woman who loved a challenge. In Manila she handled a difficult role with enthusiasm and tact; she relished travel to Japan and China, and a special diplomatic mission to the Vatican.

Further travel with her husband, who became Secretary of War in 1904, brought a widened interest in world politics and a cosmopolitan circle of friends. His election to the Presidency in 1908 gave her a position she had long desired.

As First Lady, she still took an interest in politics but concentrated on giving the administration a particular social brilliance. Only two months after the inauguration she suffered a severe stroke. An indomitable will had her back in command again within a year. At the New Year's reception for 1910, she appeared in white crepe embroidered with gold—a graceful figure. Her daughter left college for a year to take part in social life at the White House, and the gaiety of Helen's debut enhanced the 1910 Christmas season.

During four years famous for social events, the most outstanding was an evening garden party for several thousand guests on the Tafts' silver wedding anniversary, June 19, 1911. Mrs. Taft remembered this as "the greatest event" in her White House experience. Her own book, *Recollections of Full Years*, gives her account of a varied life. And the capital's famous Japanese cherry trees, planted around the Tidal Basin at her request, form a notable memorial.

Her public role in Washington did not end when she left the White House. In 1921 her husband was appointed Chief Justice of the United States—the position he had desired most of all—and she continued to live in the capital after his death in 1930. Retaining to the end her love of travel and of classical music, she died at her home on May 22, 1943.

"My dearest and best critic," William Howard Taft *wrote of his wife. She wore her inaugural gown and a tiara to sit for Bror Kronstrand in 1910 at her New England summer home; the artist added a White House setting.*

Ellen Louise Axson Wilson
1860-1914

"I am naturally the most unambitious of women and life in the White House has no attractions for me." Mrs. Wilson was writing to thank President Taft for advice concerning the mansion he was leaving. Two years as first lady of New Jersey had given her valuable experience in the duties of a woman whose time belongs to the people. She always played a public role with dignity and grace but never learned to enjoy it.

Those who knew her in the White House described her as calm and sweet, a motherly woman, pretty and refined. Her soft Southern voice had kept its slow drawl through many changes of residence.

Ellen Louise Axson grew up in Rome, Georgia, where her father, the Reverend S. E. Axson, was a Presbyterian minister. Thomas Woodrow Wilson first saw her when he was about six and she only a baby. In 1883, as a young lawyer from Atlanta, "Tommy" visited Rome and met "Miss Ellie Lou" again—a beautiful girl now, keeping house for a bereaved father. He thought, "what splendid laughing eyes!" Despite their instant attraction they did not marry until 1885, because she was unwilling to leave her heartbroken father.

That same year Bryn Mawr College offered Wilson a teaching position at an annual salary of $1,500. He and his bride lived near the campus, keeping her little brother with them. Humorously insisting that her own children must not be born Yankees, she went to relatives in Georgia for the birth of Margaret in 1886 and Jessie in 1887. But Eleanor was born in Connecticut, while Wilson was teaching at Wesleyan University.

His distinguished career at Princeton began in 1890, bringing his wife new social responsibilities. From such demands she took refuge, as always, in art. She had studied briefly in New York, and the quality of her paintings compares favorably with professional art of the period. She had a studio with a skylight installed at the White House in 1913, and found time for painting despite the weddings of two daughters within six months and the duties of hostess for the nation.

The Wilsons had preferred to begin the administration without an inaugural ball, and the First Lady's entertainments were simple; but her unaffected cordiality made her parties successful. In their first year she convinced her scrupulous husband that it would be perfectly proper to invite influential legislators to a private dinner, and when such an evening led to agreement on a tariff bill, he told a friend, "You see what a wise wife I have!"

Descendant of slave owners, Ellen Wilson lent her prestige to the cause of improving housing in the capital's Negro slums. Visiting dilapidated alleys, she brought them to the attention of debutantes and Congressmen. Her death spurred passage of a remedial bill she had worked for. Her health failing slowly from Bright's disease, she died serenely on August 6, 1914. On the day before her death, she made her physician promise to tell Wilson "later" that she hoped he would marry again; she murmured at the end, ". . . take good care of my husband." Struggling grimly to control his grief, Wilson took her to Rome for burial among her kin.

First wife of Woodrow Wilson, Ellen Louise Axson shared his life from his teaching days at Bryn Mawr to the Presidency. In Washington she devoted much time to humanitarian causes, particularly better housing for Negroes. She told a cousin that she wondered "how anyone who reaches middle age can bear it if she cannot feel, on looking back, that whatever mistakes she may have made she has on the whole lived for others and not for herself." In 1913 Robert Vonnoh depicted Mrs. Wilson serving tea to her three daughters, Margaret, Eleanor, and Jessie, at the artist's home in Cornish, New Hampshire. When Ellen Wilson became gravely ill in 1914, Margaret took over as official hostess.

Solace and support for a troubled President, Edith Wilson saw him through the agonies of wartime, frustrations of protracted peace negotiations, rejection of his dream for world order, illness, and death. Adolpho Muller-Ury portrayed her soon after she had entered the White House, early in 1916.

Edith Bolling Galt Wilson
1872-1961

"Secret President," "first woman to run the government"—so legend has labeled a First Lady whose role gained unusual significance when her husband suffered prolonged and disabling illness. A happy, protected childhood and first marriage had prepared Edith Wilson for the duties of helpmate and hostess; widowhood had taught her something of business matters.

Descendant of Virginia aristocracy, she was born in Wytheville in 1872, seventh among eleven children of Sallie White and Judge William Holcombe Bolling. Until the age of 12 she never left the town; at 15 she went to Martha Washington College to study music, with a second year at a smaller school in Richmond.

Visiting a married sister in Washington, pretty young Edith met a businessman named Norman Galt; in 1896 they were married. For 12 years she lived as a contented (though childless) young matron in the capital, with vacations abroad. In 1908 her husband died unexpectedly. Shrewdly, Edith Galt chose a good manager who operated the family's jewelry firm with financial success.

By a quirk of fate and a chain of friendships, Mrs. Galt met the bereaved President, still mourning profoundly for his first wife. A man who depended on feminine companionship, the lonely Wilson took an instant liking to Mrs. Galt, charming and intelligent and unusually pretty. Admiration changed swiftly to love. In proposing to her, he made the poignant statement that "in this place time is not measured by weeks, or months, or years, but by deep human experiences. . . ." They were married privately on December 18, 1915, at her home; and after they returned from a brief honeymoon in Virginia, their happiness made a vivid impression on their friends and White House staff.

Though the new First Lady had sound qualifications for the role of hostess, the social aspect of the administration was overshadowed by the war in Europe and abandoned after the United States entered the conflict in 1917. Edith Wilson submerged her own life in her husband's, trying to keep him fit under tremendous strain. She accompanied him to Europe when the Allies conferred on terms of peace.

Wilson returned to campaign for Senate approval of the peace treaty and the League of Nations Covenant. His health failed in September 1919; a stroke left him partly paralyzed. His constant attendant, Mrs. Wilson took over many routine duties and details of government. But she did not initiate programs or make major decisions, and she did not try to control the executive branch. She selected matters for her husband's attention and let everything else go to the heads of departments or remain in abeyance. Her "stewardship," she called this. And in *My Memoir*, published in 1939, she stated emphatically that her husband's doctors had urged this course upon her.

In 1921, the Wilsons retired to a comfortable home in Washington, where he died three years later. A highly respected figure in the society of the capital, Mrs. Wilson lived on to ride in President Kennedy's inaugural parade. She died later in 1961: on December 28, the anniversary of her famous husband's birth.

Florence Kling Harding
1860-1924

Daughter of the richest man in a small town—Amos Kling, a successful business-man—Florence Mabel Kling was born in Marion, Ohio, in 1860, to grow up in a setting of wealth, position, and privilege. Much like her strong-willed father in temperament, she developed a self-reliance rare in girls of that era.

A music course at the Cincinnati Conservatory completed her education. When only 19, she eloped with Henry De Wolfe, a neighbor two years her senior. He proved a spendthrift and a heavy drinker who soon deserted her, so she returned to Marion with her baby son. Refusing to live at home, she rented rooms and earned her own money by giving piano lessons to children of the neighborhood. She divorced De Wolfe in 1886 and resumed her maiden name; he died at age 35.

Warren G. Harding had come to Marion when only 16 and, showing a flair for newspaper work, had managed to buy the little *Daily Star*. When he met Florence a courtship quickly developed. Over Amos Kling's angry opposition they were married in 1891, in a house that Harding had planned, and this remained their home for the rest of their lives. (They had no children.)

Mrs. Harding soon took over the *Star's* circulation department, spanking news-boys when necessary. "No pennies escaped her," a friend recalled, and the paper prospered while its owner's political success increased. As he rose through Ohio politics and became a United States Senator, his wife directed all her acumen to his career. He became Republican nominee for President in 1920 and "the Duchess," as he called her, worked tirelessly for his election. In her own words: "I have only one real hobby—my husband."

She had never been a guest at the White House; and former President Taft, meeting the President-elect and Mrs. Harding, discussed its social customs with her and stressed the value of ceremony. Writing to Nellie, he concluded that the new First Lady was "a nice woman" and would "readily adapt herself."

When Mrs. Harding moved into the White House, she opened mansion and grounds to the public again—both had been closed throughout President Wilson's illness. She herself suffered from a chronic kidney ailment, but she threw herself into the job of First Lady with energy and willpower. Garden parties for veterans were regular events on a crowded social calendar. The President and his wife relaxed at poker parties in the White House library, where liquor was available although the Eighteenth Amendment made it illegal.

Mrs. Harding always liked to travel with her husband. She was with him in the summer of 1923 when he died unexpectedly in California, shortly before the public learned of the major scandals facing his administration.

With astonishing fortitude she endured the long train ride to Washington with the President's body, the state funeral at the Capitol, the last service and burial at Marion. She died in Marion on November 21, 1924, surviving Warren Harding by little more than a year of illness and sorrow.

*"The Duchess," her husband called Florence Harding. Her drive and deter-
mination helped put the 29th President in the White House in 1921. There,
in the Queens' Bedroom, hangs this portrait from life by Philip de László.*

Grace Anna Goodhue Coolidge
1879-1957

For her "fine personal influence exerted as First Lady of the Land," Grace Coolidge received a gold medal from the National Institute of Social Sciences. In 1931 she was voted one of America's twelve greatest living women.

She had grown up in the Green Mountain city of Burlington, Vermont, only child of Andrew and Lemira B. Goodhue, born in 1879. While still a girl she heard of a school for deaf children in Northampton, Massachusetts, and eventually decided to share its challenging work. She graduated from the University of Vermont in 1902 and went to teach at the Clarke School for the Deaf that autumn.

In Northampton she met Calvin Coolidge; they belonged to the same boating, picnicking, whist-club set, composed largely of members of the local Congregational Church. In October 1905 they were married at her parents' home. They lived modestly; they moved into half of a duplex two weeks before their first son was born, and she budgeted expenses well within the income of a struggling small-town lawyer.

To Grace Coolidge may be credited a full share in her husband's rise in politics. She worked hard, kept up appearances, took her part in town activities, attended her church, and offset his shyness with a gay friendliness. She bore a second son in 1908, and it was she who played backyard baseball with the boys. As Coolidge was rising to the rank of governor, the family kept the duplex; he rented a dollar-and-a-half room in Boston and came home on weekends.

In 1921, as wife of the Vice President, Grace Coolidge went from her housewife's routine into Washington society and quickly became the most popular woman in the capital. Her zest for life and her innate simplicity charmed even the most critical. Stylish clothes—a frugal husband's one indulgence—set off her good looks.

After Harding's death, she planned the new administration's social life as her husband wanted it: unpretentious but dignified. Her time and her friendliness now belonged to the nation, and she was generous with both. As she wrote later, she was "I, and yet, not I—this was the wife of the President of the United States and she took precedence over me. . . ." Under the sorrow of her younger son's sudden death at 16, she never let grief interfere with her duties as First Lady. Tact and gaiety made her one of the most popular hostesses of the White House, and she left Washington in 1929 with the country's respect and love.

For greater privacy in Northampton, the Coolidges bought "The Beeches," a large house with spacious grounds. Calvin Coolidge died there in 1933. He had summed up their marriage in his *Autobiography:* "For almost a quarter of a century she has borne with my infirmities, and I have rejoiced in her graces." After his death she sold The Beeches, bought a smaller house, and in time undertook new ventures she had longed to try: her first airplane ride, her first trip to Europe. She kept her aversion to publicity and her sense of fun until her death in 1957. Her chief activity as she grew older was serving as a trustee of the Clarke School; her great pleasure was the family of her surviving son, John.

First as a Vice President's wife, then as First Lady, Grace Goodhue Coolidge brought to Washington society the charm and simplicity of her New England upbringing and her love of people, outdoor activity, and animals. Howard Chandler Christy portrayed her in 1924 with her famous collie Rob Roy.

Lou Henry Hoover
1874-1944

Admirably equipped to preside at the White House, Lou Henry Hoover brought to it long experience as wife of a man eminent in public affairs at home and abroad. She had shared his interests since they met in a geology lab at Leland Stanford University. She was a freshman, he a senior, and he was fascinated, as he declared later, "by her whimsical mind, her blue eyes and a broad grinnish smile."

Born in Iowa, in 1874, she grew up there for ten years. Then her father, Charles D. Henry, decided that the climate of southern California would favor the health of his wife, Florence. He took his daughter on camping trips in the hills—her greatest pleasures in her early teens. Lou became a fine horsewoman; she hunted, and preserved specimens with the skill of a taxidermist; she developed an enthusiam for rocks, minerals, and mining. She entered Stanford in 1894—"slim and supple as a reed," a classmate recalled, with a "wealth of brown hair"—and completed her course before marrying Herbert Hoover in 1899.

The newlyweds left at once for China, where he won quick recognition as a mining engineer. His career took them about the globe—Ceylon, Burma, Siberia, Australia, Egypt, Japan, Europe—while her talent for homemaking eased their time in a dozen foreign lands. Two sons, Herbert and Allan, were born during this adventurous life, which made their father a youthful millionaire.

During World War I, while Hoover earned world fame administering emergency relief programs, she was often with him but spent some time with the boys in California. In 1919 she saw construction begin for a long-planned home in Palo Alto. In 1921, however, his appointment as Secretary of Commerce took the family to Washington. There she spent eight years busy with the social duties of a Cabinet wife and an active participation in the Girl Scout movement, including service as its president.

The Hoovers moved into the White House in 1929, and the First Lady welcomed visitors with poise and dignity throughout the administration. However, when the first day of 1933 dawned, Mr. and Mrs. Hoover were away on holiday. Their absence ended the New Year's Day tradition of the public being greeted personally by the President at a reception in the Executive Mansion.

Mrs. Hoover paid with her own money the cost of reproducing furniture owned by Monroe for a period sitting room in the White House. She also restored Lincoln's study for her husband's use. She dressed handsomely; she "never fitted more perfectly into the White House picture than in her formal evening gown," remarked one secretary. The Hoovers entertained elegantly, using their own private funds for social events while the country suffered worsening economic depression.

In 1933 they retired to Palo Alto, but maintained an apartment in New York. Mr. Hoover learned the full lavishness of his wife's charities only after her death there on January 7, 1944; she had helped the education, he said, "of a multitude of boys and girls." In retrospect he stated her ideal for the position she had held: "a symbol of everything wholesome in American life."

Perfectionist of hospitality, Lou Hoover as First Lady considered formal entertaining a duty to the American people. For the White House Collection, Richard M. Brown copied a 1932 portrait from life by Philip de László.

Douglas Chandor's portrait of Eleanor Roosevelt at age 65 captures a range of moods and suggests her astonishing energy. She devoted a long career to victims of poverty, prejudice, and war. Painfully shy and self-conscious in her youth, often a controversial figure in the role of President's wife, she won international respect in later years as "First Lady of the World."

Anna Eleanor Roosevelt Roosevelt
1884-1962

A shy, awkward child, starved for recognition and love, Eleanor Roosevelt grew into a woman with great sensitivity to the underprivileged of all creeds, races, and nations. Her constant work to improve their lot made her one of the most loved — and for some years one of the most reviled — women of her generation.

She was born in New York City on October 11, 1884, daughter of lovely Anna Hall and Elliott Roosevelt, younger brother of Theodore. When her mother died in 1892, the children went to live with Grandmother Hall; her adored father died only two years later. Attending a distinguished school in England gave her, at 15, her first chance to develop self-confidence among other girls.

Tall, slender, graceful of figure but apprehensive at the thought of being a wall-flower, she returned for a debut that she dreaded. In her circle of friends was a distant cousin, handsome young Franklin Delano Roosevelt. They became engaged in 1903 and were married in 1905, with her uncle the President giving the bride away. Within eleven years Eleanor bore six children; one son died in infancy. "I suppose I was fitting pretty well into the pattern of a fairly conventional, quiet, young society matron," she wrote later in her autobiography.

In Albany, where Franklin served in the state Senate from 1910 to 1913, Eleanor started her long career as political helpmate. She gained a knowledge of Washington and its ways while he served as Assistant Secretary of the Navy. When he was stricken with poliomyelitis in 1921, she tended him devotedly. She became active in the women's division of the State Democratic Committee to keep his interest in politics alive. From his successful campaign for governor in 1928 to the day of his death, she dedicated her life to his purposes. She became eyes and ears for him, a trusted and tireless reporter.

When Mrs. Roosevelt came to the White House in 1933, she understood social conditions better than any of her predecessors and she transformed the role of First Lady accordingly. She never shirked official entertaining; she greeted thousands with charming friendliness. She also broke precedent to hold press conferences, travel to all parts of the country, give lectures and radio broadcasts, and express her opinions candidly in a daily syndicated newspaper column, "My Day."

This made her a tempting target for political enemies but her integrity, her graciousness, and her sincerity of purpose endeared her personally to many — from heads of state to servicemen she visited abroad during World War II. As she had written wistfully at 14: ". . . no matter how plain a woman may be if truth & loyalty are stamped upon her face all will be attracted to her. . . ."

After the President's death in 1945 she returned to a cottage at his Hyde Park estate; she told reporters: "the story is over." Within a year, however, she began her service as American spokesman in the United Nations. She continued a vigorous career until her strength began to wane in 1962. She died in New York City that November, and was buried at Hyde Park beside her husband.

Elizabeth Virginia Wallace Truman
1885-1982

Whistle-stopping in 1948, President Harry Truman often ended his campaign talk by introducing his wife as "the Boss" and his daughter, Margaret, as "the Boss's Boss," and they smiled and waved as the train picked up steam. The sight of that close-knit family gallantly fighting against such long odds had much to do with his surprise victory at the polls that November.

Strong family ties in the southern tradition had always been important around Independence, Missouri, where a baby girl was born to Margaret ("Madge") Gates and David Wallace on February 13, 1885. Christened Elizabeth Virginia, she grew up as "Bess." Harry Truman, whose family moved to town in 1890, always kept his first impression of her—"golden curls" and "the most beautiful blue eyes." A relative said, "there never was but one girl in the world" for him. They attended the same schools from fifth grade through high school.

In recent years their daughter has written a vivid sketch of Bess as a girl: "a marvelous athlete—the best third baseman in Independence, a superb tennis player, a tireless ice skater—and she was pretty besides." She also had many "strong opinions. . . . and no hesitation about stating them Missouri style—straight from the shoulder."

For Bess and Harry, World War I altered a deliberate courtship. He proposed and they became engaged before Lieutenant Truman left for the battlefields of France in 1918. They were married in June 1919; they lived in Mrs. Wallace's home, where Mary Margaret was born in 1924.

When Harry Truman became active in politics, Mrs. Truman traveled with him and shared his platform appearances as the public had come to expect a candidate's wife to do. His election to the Senate in 1934 took the family to Washington. Reluctant to be a public figure herself, she always shared his thoughts and interests in private. When she joined his office staff as a secretary, he said, she earned "every cent I pay her." His wartime role as chairman of a special committee on defense spending earned him national recognition—and a place on the Democratic ticket as President Roosevelt's fourth-term running mate. Three months after their inauguration Roosevelt was dead. On April 12, 1945, Harry Truman took the President's oath of office—and Bess, who managed to look on with composure, was the new First Lady.

In the White House, its lack of privacy was distasteful to her. As her husband put it later, she was "not especially interested" in the "formalities and pomp or the artificiality which, as we had learned . . . , inevitably surround the family of the President." Though she conscientiously fulfilled the social obligations of her position, she did only what was necessary. While the mansion was rebuilt during the second term, the Trumans lived in Blair House and kept social life to a minimum.

They returned to Independence in 1953. After her husband's death in 1972, Mrs. Truman continued to live in the family home. There she enjoyed visits from Margaret and her husband, Clifton Daniel, and their four sons. She died in 1982 and was buried beside her husband in the courtyard of the Harry S. Truman Library.

Dignified and witty Bess Truman kept the original painting of this White House replica in her Missouri home. Her daughter, Margaret Truman Daniel, once described her as "a warmhearted, kind lady, with a robust sense of humor."

Mamie Geneva Doud Eisenhower
1896-1979

Mamie Eisenhower's bangs and sparkling blue eyes were as much trademarks of an administration as the President's famous grin. Her outgoing manner, her feminine love of pretty clothes and jewelry, and her obvious pride in husband and home made her a very popular First Lady.

Born in Boone, Iowa, Mamie Geneva Doud moved with her family to Colorado when she was seven. Her father retired from business, and Mamie and her three sisters grew up in a large house in Denver. During winters the family made long visits to relatives in the milder climate of San Antonio, Texas.

There, in 1915, at Fort Sam Houston, Mamie met Dwight D. Eisenhower, a young second lieutenant on his first tour of duty. She drew his attention instantly, he recalled: "a vivacious and attractive girl, smaller than average, saucy in the look about her face and in her whole attitude." On St. Valentine's Day in 1916 he gave her a miniature of his West Point class ring to seal a formal engagement; they were married at the Doud home in Denver on July 1.

For years Mamie Eisenhower's life followed the pattern of other Army wives: a succession of posts in the United States, in the Panama Canal Zone; duty in France, in the Philippines. She once estimated that in 37 years she had unpacked her household at least 27 times. Each move meant another step up the career ladder for her husband, with increasing responsibilities for her.

The first son Doud Dwight or "Icky," who was born in 1917, died of scarlet fever in 1921. A second child, John, was born in 1922 in Denver. Like his father he had a career in the Army; later he became an author and served as ambassador to Belgium.

During World War II, while promotion and fame came to "Ike," his wife lived in Washington. After he became president of Columbia University in 1948, the Eisenhowers purchased a farm at Gettysburg, Pennsylvania. It was the first home they had ever owned. His duties as commander of North Atlantic Treaty Organization forces— and hers as his hostess at a chateau near Paris—delayed work on their dream home, finally completed in 1955. They celebrated with a housewarming picnic for the staff from their last temporary quarters: the White House.

When Eisenhower had campaigned for President, his wife cheerfully shared his travels; when he was inaugurated in 1953, the American people warmly welcomed her as First Lady. Diplomacy—and air travel—in the postwar world brought changes in their official hospitality. The Eisenhowers entertained an unprecedented number of heads of state and leaders of foreign governments, and Mamie's evident enjoyment of her role endeared her to her guests and to the public.

In 1961 the Eisenhowers returned to Gettysburg for eight years of contented retirement together. After her husband's death in 1969, Mamie continued to live on the farm, devoting more of her time to her family and friends. Mamie Eisenhower died on November 1, 1979. She is buried beside her husband in a small chapel on the grounds of the Eisenhower Library in Abilene, Kansas.

Her famed and favorite pink casts a soft glow from Mrs. Eisenhower's rhinestone-studded inaugural gown. After many separations in Army life, she and the President happily resided in the White House for eight years.

Jacqueline Kennedy, portrayed by Aaron Shikler in 1970, stirred national interest in obtaining antiques and works of art for the White House. She planned the first historical guidebook of the mansion for its many visitors.

Jacqueline Lee Bouvier Kennedy Onassis
1929-1994

The inauguration of John F. Kennedy in 1961 brought to the White House and to the heart of the nation a beautiful young wife and the first young children of a President in half a century.

She was born Jacqueline Lee Bouvier, daughter of John Vernon Bouvier III and his wife, Janet Lee. Her early years were divided between New York City and East Hampton, Long Island, where she learned to ride almost as soon as she could walk. She was educated at the best of private schools; she wrote poems and stories, drew illustrations for them, and studied ballet. Her mother, who had obtained a divorce, married Hugh D. Auchincloss in 1942 and brought her two girls to "Merrywood," his home near Washington, D. C., with summers spent at his estate in Newport, Rhode Island. Jacqueline was dubbed "the Debutante of the year" for the 1947-1948 season, but her social success did not keep her from continuing her education. As a Vassar student she traveled extensively, and she spent her junior year in France before graduating from George Washington University. These experiences left her with a great empathy for people of foreign countries, especially the French.

In Washington she took a job as "inquiring photographer" for a local newspaper. Her path soon crossed that of Senator Kennedy, who had the reputation of being the most eligible bachelor in the capital. Their romance progressed slowly and privately, but their wedding at Newport in 1953 attracted nationwide publicity.

With marriage "Jackie" had to adapt herself to the new role of wife to one of the country's most energetic political figures. Her own public appearances were highly successful, but limited in number. After the sadness of a miscarriage and the stillbirth of a daughter, Caroline Bouvier was born in 1957; John Jr. was born between the election of 1960 and Inauguration Day. Patrick Bouvier, born prematurely on August 7, 1963, died two days later.

To the role of First Lady, Jacqueline Kennedy brought beauty, intelligence, and cultivated taste. Her interest in the arts, publicized by press and television, inspired an attention to culture never before evident at a national level. She devoted much time and study to making the White House a museum of American history and decorative arts as well as a family residence of elegance and charm. But she defined her major role as "to take care of the President" and added that "if you bungle raising your children, I don't think whatever else you do well matters very much."

Mrs. Kennedy's gallant courage during the tragedy of her husband's assassination won her the admiration of the world. Thereafter it seemed the public would never allow her the privacy she desired for herself and her children. She moved to New York City; and in 1968 she married the wealthy Greek businessman Aristotle Onassis, 23 years her senior, who died in March 1975. From 1978 until her death in 1994, Mrs. Onassis worked in New York City as an editor for Doubleday. At her funeral her son described three of her attributes: "love of words, the bonds of home and family, and her spirit of adventure."

Claudia Taylor (Lady Bird) Johnson
1912-

Christened Claudia Alta Taylor when she was born in a country mansion near Karnack, Texas, she received her nickname "Lady Bird" as a small child; and as Lady Bird she is known and loved throughout America today. Perhaps that name was prophetic, as there has seldom been a First Lady so attuned to nature and the importance of conserving the environment.

Her mother, Minnie Pattillo Taylor, died when Lady Bird was five, so she was reared by her father, her aunt, and family servants. From her father, Thomas Jefferson Taylor, who had prospered, she learned much about the business world. An excellent student, she also learned to love classical literature. At the University of Texas she earned bachelor's degrees in arts and in journalism.

In 1934 Lady Bird met Lyndon Baines Johnson, then a Congressional secretary visiting Austin on official business; he promptly asked her for a date, which she accepted. He courted her from Washington with letters, telegrams, and telephone calls. Seven weeks later he was back in Texas; he proposed to her and she accepted. In her own words: "Sometimes Lyndon simply takes your breath away." They were married in November 1934.

The years that followed were devoted to Lyndon's political career, with "Bird" as partner, confidante, and helpmate. She helped keep his Congressional office open during World War II when he volunteered for naval service; and in 1955, when he had a severe heart attack, she helped his staff keep things running smoothly until he could return to his post as Majority Leader of the Senate. He once remarked that voters "would happily have elected her over me."

After repeated miscarriages, she gave birth to Lynda Bird (now Mrs. Charles S. Robb) in 1944; Luci Baines (Mrs. Ian Turpin) was born three years later.

In the election of 1960, Lady Bird successfully stumped for Democratic candidates across 35,000 miles of campaign trail. As wife of the Vice President, she became an ambassador of goodwill by visiting 33 foreign countries. Moving to the White House after Kennedy's murder, she did her best to ease a painful transition. She soon set her own stamp of Texas hospitality on social events, but these were not her chief concern. She created a First Lady's Committee for a More Beautiful Capital, then expanded her program to include the entire nation. She took a highly active part in her husband's war-on-poverty program, especially the Head Start project for preschool children.

When the Presidential term ended, the Johnsons returned to Texas, where he died in 1973. Mrs. Johnson's *White House Diary*, published in 1970, and a 1981 documentary film, *The First Lady, A Portrait of Lady Bird Johnson*, give sensitive and detailed views of her contributions to the President's Great Society administration. Today Lady Bird leads a life devoted to her husband's memory, her children, and seven grandchildren. She still supports causes dear to her—notably the National Wildflower Research Center, which she founded in 1982, and The Lyndon Baines Johnson Library. She also serves on the Board of the National Geographic Society as a trustee emeritus.

Flower- and wilderness-lover, Lady Bird Johnson sponsored a beautification project that came to include the nation's cities and highways. "A woman of great depth and excellent judgment," President Johnson described her.

While First Lady, Pat Nixon traveled over the world more than any of her predecessors, alone or with her husband. She encouraged volunteer work— "individual attention and love and concern"—to help the less fortunate.

Patricia Ryan Nixon
1912-1993

Born Thelma Catherine Ryan on March 16 in Ely, Nevada, "Pat" Nixon acquired her nickname within hours. Her father, William Ryan, called her his "St. Patrick's babe in the morn" when he came home from the mines before dawn.

Soon the family moved to California and settled on a small truck farm near Los Angeles—a life of hard work with few luxuries. Her mother, Kate Halberstadt Bender Ryan, died in 1925; at 13 Pat assumed all the household duties for her father and two older brothers. At 18, she lost her father after nursing him through months of illness. Left on her own and determined to continue her education, she worked her way through the University of Southern California. She held part-time jobs on campus, as a sales clerk in a fashionable department store, and as an extra in the movies—and she graduated cum laude in 1937.

She accepted a position as a high-school teacher in Whittier; and there she met Richard Nixon, who had come home from Duke University Law School to establish a practice. They became acquainted at a Little Theater group when they were cast in the same play, and were married on June 21, 1940.

During World War II, she worked as a government economist while he served in the Navy. She campaigned at his side in 1946 when he entered politics, running successfully for Congress, and afterward. Within six years she saw him elected to the House, the Senate, and the Vice Presidency on the ticket with Dwight D. Eisenhower. Despite the demands of official life, the Nixons were devoted parents to their two daughters, Tricia (now Mrs. Edward Cox), and Julie (now Mrs. David Eisenhower).

A tireless campaigner when he ran unsuccessfully for President in 1960, she was at his side when he ran again in 1968—and won. She had once remarked succinctly, "It takes heart to be in political life."

Pat Nixon used her position as First Lady to encourage volunteer service—"the spirit of people helping people." She invited hundreds of families to nondenominational Sunday services in the East Room. She instituted a series of performances by artists in varied American traditions—from opera to bluegrass. Mrs. Nixon took quiet pride in adding 600 paintings and antiques to the White House Collection.

She had shared her husband's journeys abroad in his Vice Presidential years, and she continued the practice during his Presidency. Her travels included the historic visit to the People's Republic of China and the summit meeting in the Soviet Union. Her first solo trip was a journey of compassion to take relief supplies to earthquake victims in Peru. Later she visited Africa and South America with the unique diplomatic standing of Personal Representative of the President. Always she was a charming envoy.

Mrs. Nixon met the troubled days of Watergate with dignity. "I love my husband," she said, "I believe in him, and I am proud of his accomplishments." She died at home in Park Ridge, New Jersey, on June 22, 1993. Her husband followed her in death ten months later. She and the former President are buried at the Richard Nixon Library and Birthplace in Yorba Linda, California.

Once a professional dancer with Martha Graham and a teacher of dance to underprivileged youngsters, Betty Ford continues her support of dance and encourages the other arts. She staunchly advocates women's rights as well.

Elizabeth Bloomer Ford
1918-

In 25 years of political life, Betty Bloomer Ford did not expect to become First Lady. As wife of Representative Gerald R. Ford, she looked forward to his retirement and more time together. In late 1973 his selection as Vice President was a surprise to her. She was just becoming accustomed to their new roles when he became President upon Mr. Nixon's resignation in August 1974.

Born Elizabeth Anne Bloomer in Chicago, she grew up in Grand Rapids, Michigan, and graduated from high school there. She studied modern dance at Bennington College in Vermont, decided to make it a career, and became a member of Martha Graham's noted concert group in New York City, supporting herself as a fashion model for the John Robert Powers firm.

Close ties with her family and her hometown took her back to Grand Rapids, where she became fashion coordinator for a department store. She also organized her own dance group and taught dance to handicapped children.

Her first marriage, at age 24, ended in divorce five years later on the grounds of incompatibility. Not long afterward she began dating Jerry Ford, football hero, graduate of the University of Michigan and Yale Law School, and soon a candidate for Congress. They were married during the 1948 campaign; he won his election; and the Fords lived in the Washington area for nearly three decades thereafter.

Their four children—Michael, Jack, Steven, and Susan—were born in the next ten years. As her husband's political career became more demanding, Betty Ford found herself shouldering many of the family responsibilities. She supervised the home, did the cooking, undertook volunteer work, and took part in the activities of "House wives" and "Senate wives" for Congressional and Republican clubs. In addition, she was an effective campaigner for her husband.

Betty Ford faced her new life as First Lady with dignity and serenity. She accepted it as a challenge. "I like challenges very much," she said. She had the self-confidence to express herself with humor and forthrightness whether speaking to friends or to the public. Forced to undergo radical surgery for breast cancer in 1974, she reassured many troubled women by discussing her ordeal openly. She explained that "maybe if I as First Lady could talk about it candidly and without embarrassment, many other people would be able to as well." As soon as possible, she resumed her duties as hostess at the Executive Mansion and her role as a public-spirited citizen. She did not hesitate to state her views on controversial issues such as the Equal Rights Amendment, which she strongly supported.

From their home in California, she was equally frank about her successful battle against dependency on drugs and alcohol. She helped establish the Betty Ford Center for treatment of this problem at the Eisenhower Medical Center in Rancho Mirage.

She has described the role of First Lady as "much more of a 24-hour job than anyone would guess" and says of her predecessors: "Now that I realize what they've had to put up with, I have new respect and admiration for every one of them."

For many years, Rosalynn Carter has taken an active interest in volunteer work and in helping the mentally ill, the elderly, the handicapped, and the poor. The shy girl from Plains became a determined campaigner for her husband and called herself "more a political partner than a political wife." She used her influence as First Lady in behalf of women's rights. In 1980 the District of Columbia honored Mrs. Carter for her "commitment . . . to build a more caring society."

Rosalynn Smith Carter
1927-

"She's the girl I want to marry," Jimmy Carter told his mother after his first date with 17-year-old Rosalynn Smith, who had grown up as a friend and neighbor of the Carter family in Plains, Georgia.

Born in Plains on August 18, 1927, Rosalynn was the first of four children in the family of Allethea Murray Smith and Wilburn Edgar Smith. She grew up in a small-town atmosphere that nurtured strong ties to family and dedication to church and community. When she was 13, her father died and her mother became a dressmaker to help support the family. As the oldest child, Rosalynn worked beside her mother, helping with the sewing, the housekeeping, and the other children.

Times were difficult, but Rosalynn completed high school and enrolled in Georgia Southwestern College at Americus. In 1945, after her freshman year, she first dated Jimmy Carter, who was home from the U. S. Naval Academy at Annapolis. Their romance progressed, and in 1946 they were married.

The young couple went to Norfolk, Virginia, Ensign Carter's first duty station after graduation. The Navy kept them on the move. Their sons were born in different places: John William in Virginia, James Earl III in Hawaii, and Donnel Jeffrey in Connecticut. The Carters' only daughter, Amy Lynn, was born in Georgia in 1967.

When his father died in 1953, Jimmy left the service, and the Carters returned to Plains to run the family business. Managing the accounts of the peanut, fertilizer, and seed enterprise, Rosalynn soon found herself working full-time.

Jimmy entered politics in 1962, winning a seat in the Georgia Senate. Rosalynn, an important member of his campaign team, helped develop support for her husband's successful bid for the governorship of Georgia in 1970. During his Presidential campaigns, Rosalynn traveled independently throughout the United States. Her belief in her husband's ability to lead the nation was communicated in a quiet, friendly manner that made her an effective campaigner.

A skillful speaker and a hardworking First Lady, Mrs. Carter managed routine duties and special projects in her office in the East Wing. She attended Cabinet meetings and major briefings, frequently represented the Chief Executive at ceremonial occasions, and served as the President's personal emissary to Latin American countries.

As First Lady, she focused national attention on the performing arts. She invited to the White House leading classical artists from around the world, as well as traditional American artists. She also took a strong interest in programs to aid mental health, the community, and the elderly. From 1977 to 1978, she served as the Honorary Chairperson of the President's Commission on Mental Health.

After returning home, Mrs. Carter wrote her autobiography, *First Lady From Plains*, published in 1984. She is a director of the Carter Center, where she manages an active mental health program and works with human rights, conflict resolution, and childhood immunization. She also shares her community service talents with Habitat for Humanity, an organization that builds homes for the underprivileged.

Nancy Davis Reagan
1923-

"My life really began when I married my husband," says Nancy Reagan, who in the 1950's happily gave up an acting career for a permanent role as the wife of Ronald Reagan and mother to their children. Her story actually begins in New York City, her birthplace. She was born on July 6, 1923, according to her autobiography *Nancy*, published in 1980. When the future First Lady was six, her mother, Edith—a stage actress—married Dr. Loyal Davis, a neurosurgeon. Dr. Davis adopted Nancy, and she grew up in Chicago. It was a happy time: summer camp, tennis, swimming, dancing. She received her formal education at Girls' Latin School and at Smith College in Massachusetts, where she majored in theater.

Soon after graduation she became a professional actress. She toured with a road company, then landed a role on Broadway in the hit musical *Lute Song*. More parts followed. One performance drew an offer from Hollywood. Billed as Nancy Davis, she performed in 11 films from 1949 to 1956. Her first screen role was in *Shadow on the Wall*. Other releases included *The Next Voice You Hear* and *East Side, West Side*. In her last movie, *Hellcats of the Navy*, she played opposite her husband.

She had met Ronald Reagan in 1951, when he was president of the Screen Actors Guild. The following year they were married in a simple ceremony in Los Angeles in the Little Brown Church in the Valley. Mrs. Reagan soon retired from making movies so she "could be the wife I wanted to be. . . . A woman's real happiness and real fulfillment come from within the home with her husband and children," she says. President and Mrs. Reagan have a daughter, Patricia Ann, and a son, Ronald Prescott.

While her husband was Governor of California from 1967 to 1975, she worked with numerous charitable groups. She spent many hours visiting veterans, the elderly, and the emotionally and physically handicapped. These people continued to interest her as First Lady. She gave her support to the Foster Grandparent Program, the subject of her 1982 book, *To Love A Child*. Increasingly, she has concentrated on the fight against drug and alcohol abuse among young people. She visited prevention and rehabilitation centers, and in 1985 she held a conference at the White House for First Ladies of 17 countries to focus international attention on this problem.

Mrs. Reagan shared her lifelong interest in the arts with the nation by using the Executive Mansion as a showcase for talented young performers in the PBS television series "In Performance at the White House." In her first year in the mansion she directed a major renovation of the second- and third-floor quarters.

Now living in retirement with her husband in California, she continues to work on her campaign to teach children to "just say no" to drugs, though her husband and her home remain her first priority. In her book *My Turn*, published in 1989, she gives her own account of her life in the White House. Through the joys and sorrows of those days, including the assassination attempt on her husband, Nancy Reagan held fast to her belief in love, honesty, and selflessness. "The ideals have endured because they are right and are no less right today than yesterday."

Nancy Davis Reagan focused national attention on the problem of drug abuse in young people. Artist Aaron Shikler portrays her in the Red Room, her favorite of the White House state rooms, by a door leading into the State Dining Room.

Barbara Pierce Bush
1925-

Rarely has a First Lady been greeted by the American people and the press with the approbation and warmth accorded to Barbara Pierce Bush. Perhaps this is prompted by the image she calls "everybody's grandmother." People are comfortable with her white hair, her warm, relaxed manner, and her keen wit. With characteristic directness, she says people like her because they know "I'm fair and I like children and I adore my husband."

Barbara was born in 1925 to Pauline and Marvin Pierce, who later became president of McCall Corporation. In the suburban town of Rye, New York, she had a happy childhood. She went to boarding school at Ashley Hall in South Carolina, and it was at a dance during Christmas vacation when she was only 16 that she met George Bush, a senior at Phillips Academy in Andover, Massachusetts. They became engaged a year and a half later, just before he went off to war as a Navy torpedo bomber pilot. By the time George returned on leave, Barbara had dropped out of Smith College. Two weeks later, on January 6, 1945, they were married.

After the war, George graduated from Yale, and they set out for Texas to start their lives together. Six children were born to them: George, Robin, Jeb, Neil, Marvin, and Dorothy. Meanwhile, George built a business in the oil industry. With Texas as home base, he then turned to politics and public service, serving as a Member of Congress, U. S. Ambassador to the United Nations, Chairman of the Republican National Committee, Chief of the U. S. Liaison Office in the People's Republic of China, Director of the Central Intelligence Agency, and later as Vice President. In those 44 years of marriage, Mrs. Bush managed 29 moves of the family.

When her husband was away, she became the family linchpin, providing everything from discipline to carpools. The death of their daughter Robin from leukemia when she was not quite four left George and Barbara Bush with a lifelong compassion. She says, "Because of Robin, George and I love every living human more."

Barbara Bush was always an asset to her husband during his campaigns for public office. Her friendly, forthright manner won her high marks from the voters and the press. As wife of the Vice President, she selected the promotion of literacy as her special cause. As First Lady, she called working for a more literate America the "most important issue we have." Involved with many organizations devoted to this cause, she became Honorary Chairman of the Barbara Bush Foundation for Family Literacy. A strong advocate of volunteerism, Mrs. Bush helped many causes—including the homeless, AIDS, the elderly, and school volunteer programs.

Today Barbara Bush lives in a home she and her husband built in Houston, Texas, where she enjoys being part of the community. Their children and grandchildren visit them often in Houston and at the family summer home in Kennebunkport, Maine. Devoted to her family, Mrs. Bush has found time to write an autobiography, to serve on the Boards of AmeriCares and the Mayo Clinic, and to continue her prominent role in the Barbara Bush Foundation.

An active volunteer for many years for the cause of literacy, Barbara Bush feels everybody should help some charitable cause. "If it worries you, then you've got to do something about it." Such sincerity has won the hearts of the nation.

Energetic First Lady Hillary Rodham Clinton juggles a heavy work agenda, ranging from performing the duties of the official White House hostess to participating in forums on women's issues. Mrs. Clinton has devoted her career to working for "America's most unprotected citizens—its children." She urges Americans "to reach across the lines that divide us not with pointing fingers but with outstretched hands. That's the kind of America I see in the future with my husband as President."

Hillary Rodham Clinton
1947-

Hillary Rodham Clinton arrived at the White House after serving as First Lady of Arkansas for 12 years. During that time she had managed many roles: wife, mother, and homemaker; full-time partner in a law firm; and chairwoman of an education committee that set public school standards in Arkansas. On many occasions Hillary Clinton has spoken about the need "to find the right balance in our lives." For her, the elements of that balance are family, work, and public service.

Hillary Diane Rodham was born in Chicago, Illinois, on October 26, 1947, daughter of Hugh and Dorothy Rodham. Her father owned a fabric store, and her mother was a full-time mother and homemaker. Mrs. Rodham encouraged Hillary to go to college and pursue a profession, even though she had never done so herself.

Hillary and her younger brothers, Hugh and Tony, grew up in Park Ridge, Illinois, as a close-knit family. Her brothers played football, while Hillary enjoyed tennis, swimming, ballet, softball, volleyball, and skating. An excellent student, she was also a Girl Scout and a member of the local Methodist youth group.

She entered Wellesley College in 1965. Graduating with honors, she moved on to Yale Law School, where she served on the Board of Editors of the *Yale Review of Law and Social Action*. While at Yale she developed her concern for protecting the interests of children and families. It was there, too, that she met Bill Clinton, a fellow student.

In 1973 Hillary became a staff attorney for the Children's Defense Fund. A year later she was recruited by the Impeachment Inquiry staff of the Judiciary Committee of the House of Representatives.

Hillary left Washington and "followed her heart to Arkansas," marrying Bill Clinton in 1975. The couple taught together on the law faculty of the University of Arkansas in Fayetteville. Their daughter, Chelsea, was born in 1980.

In Arkansas, Hillary worked tirelessly on behalf of children and families. She founded the Arkansas Advocates for Children and Families and served on the board of the Arkansas Children's Hospital. In addition to serving as chairwoman of the Arkansas Education Standards Committee, she introduced a pioneering program called the Home Instruction Program for Preschool Youngsters. It soon became a model for other states. The program sent teachers into the homes of underprivileged families to train parents to work with their children in school preparedness and literacy. In recognition of her professional and personal accomplishments, Hillary was named Arkansas' Woman of the Year in 1983 and its Young Mother of the Year in 1984.

Like her predecessors, Hillary Rodham Clinton brings her own special talents to the role of First Lady. Since her arrival at the White House, Mrs. Clinton has taken delight in using it as a showcase for the performing arts, American cuisine, and crafts. The President appointed her to head his Task Force on National Health Care Reform, one of his highest priorities on taking office. As the President remarked: "We have a First Lady of many talents…who most of all can bring people together around complex and difficult issues to hammer out consensus and get things done."

Illustrations Credits

A photographic portrait of Mrs. Clinton appears because an official painting has not yet been acquired.

Composition for *The First Ladies* by the Typographic section of National Geographic Production Services, Pre-Press Division. Printed and bound by R. R. Donnelley & Sons, Willard, Ohio.